THE PLACES YOU GO

THE PLACES YOU GO

*Caring for Your Congregation
Monday Through Saturday*

URIAS BEVERLY

ABINGDON PRESS
Nashville

THE PLACES YOU GO
CARING FOR YOUR CONGREGATION MONDAY THROUGH SATURDAY

Copyright © 2003 by Abingdon Press

All rights reserved.

This book is printed on recycled, acid-free, elemental-chlorine–free paper.

Library of Congress Cataloging-in-Publication Data

Beverly, Urias.
   The places you go : caring for your congregation Monday through Saturday / Urias Beverly.
      p. cm.
   ISBN 0-687-02554-0 (pbk., adhesive : alk. paper)
   1. Pastoral theology. 2. Theology, Practical. I. Title.

BV4011.3.B48 2004
253—dc22
                                        2003015793

All scripture quotations unless noted otherwise are taken from the *New Revised Standard Version of the Bible*, copyright 1989 by the Division of Christian Education of the National Council of the Churches of Christ in the United States of America. Used by permission. All rights reserved.

Those marked (KJV) are from the King James Version of the Bible.

Those marked (NKJV) are taken from the New King James Version. Copyright © 1982 by Thomas Nelson, Inc. Used by permission. All rights reserved.

03 04 05 06 07 08 09 10 11 12—10 9 8 7 6 5 4 3 2 1

MANUFACTURED IN THE UNITED STATES OF AMERICA

CONTENTS

110266

ONE

INTRODUCTION

Pastors must minister in a variety of settings. Each setting, whether it is a hospital room, jail, nursing home, funeral home, parishioner's home, or pastor's study, is different. Each setting brings its own unique dilemmas and rules. Even the pastor's authority will vary according to the setting, as will the expectations of the pastor and those to whom he or she is called to minister. But in all settings at all times, good pastoring requires being in relationship. While many pastors and some traditions hold that the most important gift and skill for a pastor is preaching, I, as a preacher reared in a strong preaching tradition, suggest that a sermon is only as effective as it is relational. That is, a sermon can only be effective if it is communicated, and communication comes about only when people are in a relationship.

I have personally known a number of pastors several years ago for which preaching was not their strongest gift, to put it kindly. I wondered how they could be so effective in their pastoral ministry, especially in traditions where preaching is held in high regard. I have come to learn that the secret of their success was the fact that they had solid, Christ-centered relationships with their people. Over the years they established such good relationships that the congregants tolerated their preaching shortcomings and loved them anyway. Whatever the pastor says or does, it is all about relationship, whether we are talking about relationship with God, relationship with believers within the church, or relationship with the world. But the parameters of the relationship are often defined by the setting.

I grew up in a home where affection was not demonstrated very often (I remember my mother hugging me only once in my life). My father was a pastor and ours was a very strict home. I accepted Christ at age five; I had to do it three more times before they took me seriously enough to baptize me. Shortly thereafter, when I requested the opportunity to preach, I was taken seriously at first and a time was set for me to do it. I had been preaching in the backyard for two years already, and a community delegation had come to my house asking my parents to stop me from preaching. My parents never said a word about it to me until I was ordained at twenty-four.

Like my father, I was very conservative and judgmental as I preached around the state of Indiana as a boy. By the time I was fourteen, I realized that I was not going to save the whole world as a preacher. I was already counseling with teens and parents about relationship issues, and I wanted to become a psychologist. After completing a bachelor's degree in psychology, I began studying counseling in graduate school. It was then that I became aware that psychologists often observed clients from a distance, at least in comparison to pastoral counseling. So when I entered seminary the next year, I set my major in pastoral care and counseling.

My first big lesson in counseling was to be aware of my feelings and the role feelings played in people's lives. I did not know that I had feelings for the most part; I thought when I stuffed them away they left. My next great learning was the value and the power of relationship. After six years of training in pastoral care and counseling and a lot of experience, I acquired three national certifications as chaplain, counselor, and educator of chaplains (clinical pastoral education, CPE supervisor), and received a state license as a marriage and family therapist and social worker. I have worked in the field for more than twenty-five years and have attended and led seminars and workshops nationally and internationally. I have enjoyed traveling extensively and providing leadership as president of the Association for Clinical Pastoral Education (ACPE), the association that certified me to teach pastoral care. I have published several articles in the field and have mentored several doctoral students in pastoral care.

I now direct a doctorate of ministry program at an up-and-coming seminary in Detroit and pastor a church northwest of Detroit. Although I have retired from fulltime pastoral care and supervision, I still supervise CPE students and see a few clients for counseling. During my entire institutional ministry I have always remained very involved in the parish, either as pastor or assistant pastor. I have mentored many parish pastors and counseled many pastors and their spouses. I enjoy retreat ministry and have had some memorable experiences as I continue to do that ministry. In all of the different ministries I do and have done, I find that the basic necessity is relationship. People need relationship, especially these days when phone conversations have been replaced by email; cell phones keep us from meeting new people as we travel because we continue to talk to ones we already know; and electronic technology allows students to study at a distance, so the relationships that use to be established in the classroom do not happen. We need relationship; without it there is no trust. There is no container or structure to talk about all the feelings we need to talk about.

One of my mentors shared with me what his mentor shared with him: "The only responsibility of the therapist is to show up at the appointed place and the appointed time and collect the fee." I shuddered when I first heard that. How cold can you be to show up and collect the fee? After years of reflection and experience I know what he was saying: people need someone they can trust to be there for them when they say they will be. Life is so uncertain and people are so disappointing that to be there where and when you agreed to be there is worth the fee if nothing else happens. When the minister keeps the appointment it says everything that needs to be said about the relationship. It is integrity, which is the most basic aspect of any relationship. All else that may be achieved is icing on the cake.

Recently, one of my clinical pastoral education (CPE) students, who is and has been a sensitive and caring pastor for years, reported, "Before CPE I just helped people any way I could; if a relationship happened, good, if not, well I just did the best I could. But now, since I know the value of intentionally building pastoral relationships and have learned some skills in how to develop these relationships in different settings, my ministry has improved by leaps and bounds." Too many pastors simply assume that relationship just happens and that the setting is of no consequence.

Nothing could be further from the truth. If pastoral skills are the tools that are used to give support and guidance to someone needing help, relationship is the box in which the tools are carried and the setting is like the worktable. If technique is the gasoline that powers, then the setting is the engine, and relationship is the oil that allows the parts to move smoothly to facilitate healing. If verbal and nonverbal communications are the ingredients, the setting is the *pastoral-sustaining bread,* and relationship is the yeast that makes it rise, making it light and delicious.

In this book we will look at the pastor in several different settings of his or her ministry, including the parishioner's home, hospitals, nursing homes, funeral homes, the pastor's office, and the jail. In each case the necessity and value of relationship will be lifted up with suggestions on how to develop and sustain pastoral relationships in these settings.

Each chapter will discuss how the pastor establishes rapport in the particular setting, the pastor's role and authority that may be unique to the setting, as well as appropriate rituals, etiquette, dilemmas in that setting, and then resources pastors can call upon.

We will begin by reflecting on the concept of pastor because real relationship does not happen unless we know who we are.

Relationship is about connectedness, one person being connected to another person in a way that allows both persons to share trust, warmth, challenge, peace, pain, and hope between them. We understand connectedness in terms of a part to a mechanical or electrical device; if we install the wrong part we could be in for a lot of trouble. In electronics, the wrong part could cause the device not to work at all; however, sometimes we can use a transformer to connect two different kinds of parts. In medicine, especially in blood transfusion or transplantation, an inadequate connector can be fatal. So it is with ministry: the better we know ourselves, the better we can connect to others. Sometimes knowing ourselves lets us know immediately that we cannot connect with certain people in a positive way.

What we come to know and accept about ourselves is summed up in what we call identity. As ministers, we have several identities: personal, professional, public, and private; and these often vary, depending on which type of ministry we may be doing at the time. Each of these faces and hats we wear has characteristics and boundaries that are general in nature, but specific to each person. Our identity varies according to our personality, childhood environment, education and training, life experience, and spiritual development. Our identity is like a part with a number on it. Although we like to think that we are "one size that fits all," in reality, in some cases we are a perfect fit and in others we are a disaster. The better we know our strengths and weakness, what bores us and what turns us on, what we have and what we long for, and what symptoms indicate when we have had enough, the better we will connect to others and help them get to know and accept themselves. In short, the better ministry we will be able to do.

There is another side to the pastors' identity other than the way they see themselves. It is the way they are seen by others. This is especially true of parish pastors because their relationships are long-term, they represent a long tradition, and they are highly respected by many people. Parish pastors, for all of their images of strength and being above the fray, are not as free as they may seem. They are accountable to God on the one hand and to the congregation on the other. If pastors wonder which of these identities is of greater importance, how they see themselves or how they are seen by others, I would have to say, "When a pastor is ministering to a someone, that person's perception, right or wrong, is the only reality there is at that time. We are all limited to our reality and perception. The difference is that a wise pastor realizes that and tries to compensate for it. Others simply believe *their* perception is the only way to see the issue."

I once counseled a couple who was struggling with their differences in values. The man was very intelligent and had a scientific mind. His wife was also intelligent, but much more people oriented. Whenever they would fight he would explain his position over and over again, believing that she did not understand his point of view. One day they were fighting in my office, and he kept saying, "You just don't understand." He tried one more time to explain his position. When he was finished I asked her if she heard what he had said. She repeated it back to me. I asked her if she understood the point he was making. She explained his point. I asked her if she agreed with his point of view. She replied, "No!" I then said to him, "She does understand your point, she just happens to disagree." He was totally baffled. How could she disagree with his brilliant idea!

Regardless as to how pastors see themselves, parishioners may not agree and that can be a difficult thing to overcome in a relationship. Pastors must always be thoughtful of how well they are being faithful to their calling by God, since God is the one to whom they are ultimately accountable. Their role, which God has assigned, is to give comfort, guidance, and healing. Their next concern is to satisfy their own sense of value and integrity. Finally, they must be aware of how they are seen and experienced by those they serve. It is like a juggling act to keep all of these things in constant balance. If they are not kept in balance, however, it can limit the effects of ministry and do harm to the parishioner, the pastor, and even the denomination.

After discussing the meaning of a pastoral relationship and the theology of the pastor's role in relationship to God and community, we will describe a good pastoral relationship and how it can be established generally. Each chapter thereafter will focus on pastoral relationships in more specific settings and situations.

CONCEPT OF PASTOR

The word *pastor* comes from the Greek word *poimen*, meaning a shepherd—one who tends herds or flocks (not merely one who feeds them).[1] "The word *shepherd* is used metaphorically of biblical passages such as in John 10. Ephesians 4:11 makes the point that pastors are appointed by Christ. Acts 20:28 calls pastors overseers and suggests that their responsibility is to keep watch over themselves and the flock of the Holy Spirit . . . be shepherds of the church of God. First Peter 5:2 calls for the pastor to be a shepherd of God's flock in your care serving as an overseer."[2] First Peter 2:25 depicts the shepherd as the overseer of our souls. Although the metaphor of sheep and shepherd is used extensively in Scripture, it points to intimacy in relationship, as well as mutuality (John 10), defender and advocate (Ezra 3–4), and leader (1 Sam. 17:34, 35). Today, pastors need those same relational characteristics: intimacy, mutuality, advocacy, and leadership, but, above all, pastors need to appreciate what it means to know and understand in relationship.

KNOWING AND UNDERSTANDING IN RELATIONSHIP

Knowing and understanding in relationship is also to be known and understood. Parker Palmer says it is not enough for human beings to know each other as isolated observers; they also must know each other in the context of relationship and the act of relating. He writes, "The relationships of the self require not only sensory evidence of the other, not only logical linkages of cause and effect; they also require inner understanding of the other, which comes from empathy; a sense of the other's value, which comes from love; a feel for its origins and ends, which comes from faith; and a respect for its integrity and selfhood, which comes from respecting our own."[3]

Effective pastors must first have a good grasp of their own identity—their gifts and limitations; they must also be clear about their call to ministry and thereby to whom they are accountable and from where their help comes. Second, they must realize and appreciate the vulnerability of the person who comes to them for help and the sanctity of the pastoral relationship with one of God's children. It is a good thing when pastors realize that they are vulnerable too. One of the characteristics of relationship is vulnerability. Vulnerable does not mean weak, it means being open to the possibilities of the present moment; being open to love, warmth, intimacy, and the moving of the Holy Spirit.

We must know in relationship through our capacities of empathy, intuition, compassion, and faith. Parker says, "When we allow the whole self to know in relationship, we come into a community of mutual knowing in which we will be transformed even as we transform."[4] The effective pastor does not hide behind his or her role as a pastor, God's representative, the one who has it all together, or the strong one lending a helping hand to the weak. The successful pastor is willing to risk giving himself or herself away in relationship, so that he or she can be known as much as he or she knows and so that he or she can be transformed while he or she is transforming the other. This certainly does not mean that the pastor should dump his or her stuff on the parishioner or share all of his or her shortcomings, but it does mean that the pastor should *not* try to convey that he or she has all of the answers to life's situations. There are limitations to how intimate a pastor can be with some parishioners. Some people are not intimate with anybody, including their own spouses and children; how can they be expected to be intimate with a pastor? They may have been wounded by someone and may be afraid of intimacy. This is why the pastor must be aware of how he or she is experienced by the parishioner.

There was a man who attended college with me. We may have graduated the same year; I am not sure. In college he called me Urias, as did everybody else, and I called him Bill. Later, I became an assistant pastor to the church where he was a member with a leadership role. I encouraged people there to call me Urias. Many did, but not Bill. He called me Reverend Beverly for five or six years, while I continued to call him Bill. When I asked him about it, he said he was not comfortable calling me Urias. I never mentioned it again. One day, years later, he called me Urias. Parishioners have a comfort zone and should not be urged to come out of that place until they are ready.

On the other hand, too much intimacy between pastor and parishioner can lead to other dangers. Some people are not able to distinguish professional concern, compassion, and empathy from personal love and romance. Some pastors have difficulty with this issue. It is the pastor's responsibility to set appropriate boundaries for the relationship and realize that too much self-revelation can be a problem. So there has to be a balance in how much pastors should share about themselves and how much they should remain formal in their approach to some people in some situations.

THE PASTOR AS CONNECTING LINK

Pastors connect the church or faith group with those outside the church—the world. But if a pastor is not appropriately connected and credentialed within a community of faith, it raises a serious question about the pastor's legitimacy and accountability. Because of the connection of the pastor, those with whom he or she relates are automatically brought into relationship with the body of faith and the God in whom that faith resides. According to Patton, "Pastoral counselors are representatives of the central image of life and its meaning affirmed by their religious communities. Thus pastoral counseling offers a relationship to that understanding of life and faith through the person of the pastoral counselor."[5] This is also true for parish pastors. Like the broker, the pastor brings the individual person into community with the faith group he or she represents.

Sometimes, however, the path into a faith community is nei-ther easy nor obvious. When humans experience brokenness in their lives, they often feel distant, perhaps even alienated from the faith community and especially God. Their hurt, guilt, and/or shame can make them feel unloved and unworthy of grace and reconciliation. They may come to the pastor seeking forgiveness, acceptance, healing, and/or guidance. They may also come seek-ing chastisement, condemnation, and/or vindication. It is never enough to say the right words (whatever they are) or do the right thing (whatever that is); the pastor must develop a level of trust with the parishioner so that the pastor's input will be believed and accepted. Through the relationship with the pastor, the parishioner can feel included once again in the fellowship of believers and feel the power of God's love, forgiveness, and acceptance. The brokenness is placed on the altar of redemption and God's grace restores and reconnects the longing soul with a supportive community.

LEVELS OF RELATIONSHIP

The pastoral relationship defines the responsibility and accountability of the pastor with the parishioner. In developing relationship the pastor learns what expectations the parishioner has of him or her. This knowledge shapes the attitude with which the pastor approaches the situation. It sets the stage for the trans-forming power of the gospel to take place. It sets the boundaries for interaction between the pastor and the parishioner(s). It gives identity to the pastor and parishioner and gives legitimacy to the process of interaction. It defines the pastoral intervention as dif-ferent from similar intervention processes and enhances the qual-ity of the interaction. Whether the relationship is formal or informal, the dynamics of spirituality are present and the grace of God has an acknowledged channel through which to bring about healing and wholeness. This is not to say that God confines Godself to pastors as the only means through which God's grace can be channeled; however, it is the acceptance of the parishioner that is most important. For some parishioners, the pastor is the only channel for the grace of God to be brought to them. When parishioners come for help, that is not the time to teach them that they could have found what they needed anywhere if they had just had faith. There are different levels of relationship with different people or even with the same person at different times, but they all begin in much the same way.

DEVELOPING THE PASTORAL RELATIONSHIP

I say to all of my students, "That pastoral, by definition, means relationship. There may be very good acts of kindness, caring, and healing that take place between people; but if there is no relationship, it is not pastoral, because relationship means commitment, accountability, and reciprocity. A pastoral relationship also involves commitment, accountability, and reciprocity with others and with God in a self-conscious way." Relationship means commitment to the parishioner and to the process of relating. It means accountability to God, self, parishioner, and congregation. Relationship means give and take on the part of all who are involved in the situation at hand. It is not only the parishioner that *takes* the pastor's time and energy; each parishioner *brings* something as well. I have learned much more from parishioners than I ever did in school or training. As a matter of fact, when I relate with somebody and do not feel that I have learned anything, I feel somebody has stolen something from me.

I also say to my students, "A good pastoral relationship covers a multitude of sins." My point here is that when we do the best we can to relate with others, we still make mistakes: we forget an appointment or a name, we misunderstand what the person is trying to say, or we say the wrong thing at the wrong time. If we have a good relationship the parishioner will be understanding and forgiving; if not, that may well be the end of the conversation or any other future conversation. A good relationship allows us to be human.

When an Appointment Is Called For

We all have relationships with people that serve well on a day-to-day basis, but when the special situation arises, the quality and depth of the relationship must be adjusted appropriately. The pastor cannot assume because he or she has known the parishioner for a long time that there is enough trust and respect between them to deal with the problem at hand; the current situation requires a relationship appropriate to the need. When the pastor hears those awesome words, "I need to talk to you!" an alert pastor recognizes this does not mean the usual kind of talk; this means in conversation in private with certain conditions. The conditions are spelled out in the verbal and nonverbal context of relationship in a particular setting. The parishioner may begin by saying, "We've known each other for a long time and I hate to bother you with this, but . . . " He or she may go on to say, "Now this is between you and me, right?" A new dynamic has entered a long-standing relationship and the pastor has to rise to the task of reassuring the individual that he or she is in a safe situation with the pastor.

Five Steps to a More Formal Pastoral Relationship

When setting aside time and meeting with a person or family, the pastor is developing a more formal pastoral relationship. Although there can be a variety of settings, there are five steps to this process: (1) introduction, (2) establishing rapport, (3) gathering background information, (4) spiritual diagnosis, and (5) closing.

1. The Introduction

When meeting someone for the first time it is crucial that the pastor introduce himself or herself. The introduction sets the framework for the kind of relationship that will proceed. There are several points to remember in introducing oneself; the first one is name.

Name

It is important the pastor be intentional about the name he or she gives in introducing himself or herself. What's in a name? There is an awful lot in a name: identity, intimacy, power, uniqueness, boundaries, freedom, history, potentiality—the list goes on. The pastor is the owner of his or her name. It is up to the pastor to share that name with whomever he or she decides to share it. The pastor may share his or her first name, middle name, last name, or all of the above. It should be understood that when the pastor shares his or her name with a parishioner in an introduction, it gives the parishioner the power and permission to use that name. It is a contract the pastor is making with the parishioner he or she is meeting, and it implies that the one to whom the name is given may use all or any part of that name when referring to the pastor who gave it.

When I introduce myself, I am very intentional about how much power I give to the other person in sharing my name. Since I like my first name, Urias, very much and prefer that most people address me in most situations by that name, that is usually the name that I give to people that I am meeting. However, there are times when I choose to introduce myself as Mr. Beverly. My father always introduced himself as R. W. Beverly. Only people who were very closely associated with him knew that his first name was Roy.

There is another reason I am eager to introduce myself as Urias Beverly. My concept of a pastoral relationship is that it is a mutual relationship between the pastor and the parishioner. I offer my first name as a way to suggest that this relationship be open, intimate, equal, and mutual. I could *require* the parishioner to address me as Urias by simply not sharing my last name with him or her. I have learned through years of experience that many people are uncomfortable addressing the pastor by his or her first name. I include my last name for the benefit of those people. Now that the person knows that my name is Urias Beverly, he or she has the opportunity to respond to me as Urias or as Beverly or as Urias Beverly. I will answer to any of the three—and a number of other things to which I have learned to respond over the years.

There are other considerations to address before one can decide how to introduce himself or herself. Some of the issues have to do with age, gender, race, culture, location, social expectations, professional expectations, stature, and many other things that may play into this relationship. I have often encouraged women students to not introduce themselves by their first names if they would like to gain respect as pastors. This is particularly true when they may be introducing themselves to someone who is past sixty years old and may not be accustomed to women in ministry. Since the tendency, particularly for men but not limited to men, is to address women by their first name regardless of their status. The problem may become greater if the woman student is young and/or attractive. Some people just do not take them seriously, but it is important that the relationship require the respect of the pastor as a professional person. Confining the relationship to the woman pastor's last name sends a message to the person whom she may be pastoring that she is to be taken seriously. Instead of "My name is Betty King," the woman pastor may say, "I am Ms. or Reverend King."

Age can play a large role in how a pastor introduces himself or herself. Several years ago I had a student that I will call for the sake of illustration Charlie Mendez. As you can tell by the last name, Charlie was Hispanic. He was attending seminary to become a Catholic priest. Charlie could easily pass for someone in his mid-teens—he was short, looked like he did not need to shave, and had a high tenor voice. Charlie came running to me one day in frustration and anger. He blurted out, "I am tired of people not taking me seriously as a chaplain." Charlie had just come from a patient's room where he introduced himself and asked the woman if there was anything he could do. She asked him to go and bring her a popular magazine. Charlie said okay, but he was frustrated because he felt dismissed. His face must have betrayed ill feelings, but she determined that he wanted some money, which she quickly gave him and asked him again to bring the magazine. Charlie did take to the patient the magazine she requested, but came immediately to talk to me about what had happened and why she did not relate to him as a pastor.

We talked about how he introduced himself. Charlie most often introduced himself as Charlie the chaplain. After talking about it for some time I looked at Charlie and said to him, "You look too young to get away with introducing yourself as Charlie." I suggested that he practice introducing himself as Reverend, Chaplain, or Mr. Mendez. I urged him to practice a few times so that the Mendez would come forth in a lower-pitched voice. He went away happy, realizing that he had a new tool available to him in introducing himself to people. He later reported that it worked; people seemed to have more respect for him when he did not introduce himself as Charlie.

In another situation, I had a very large student with a big voice who had been in ministry for years and he looked like it. He was accustomed to introducing himself as Pastor Williams (not his real name). He wondered why people were so eager to get rid of him, to send him to their roommate, to tell him that their own pastor was coming, or they would immediately become defensive about their participation in church activities. In a verbatim conference his peers suggested that he had frightened a woman patient. He responded that he felt she was a little intimidated by him but he had no idea why. We eventually talked about how he introduced himself. The group suggested to him that he presented too much of an authority figure given his large stature, the sound of his voice, and the way he introduced himself. They suggested to him that he use only his first name when introducing himself so that he would come across to patients in a friendlier manner.

How a pastor introduces himself or herself is a personal decision that must be made by each individual. I encourage pastors to explore ways that they introduce themselves until they find something that has the effect that they would like to have when they are establishing a pastoral relationship.

Role

The second point to consider when introducing oneself is the role that the pastor is filling. Because I am discussing role second does not necessarily mean that roles should always be the second thing to be shared with a person in introduction. It may be better to share the role first if the pastor is young or if the pastor does not fit people's expectations of what a pastor should look like. This especially applies to some young women. For others whose appearance or demeanor in itself is powerful, for example, who are middle-aged, heavy-set with gray hair and/or a big voice, and so forth, it may be more important to emphasize the name and minimize the role.

I am sure someone would argue that it is the role of pastor that makes this relationship valid. My response is when you walk like a pastor, talk like a pastor, look like a pastor, and introduce yourself as pastor, even in a gentle way, it is unlikely that the role will not be perceived by the person to whom you are introducing yourself. In other words, it is unnecessary to accent the obvious. The role of the pastor is different for every pastor and every person. When pastors are visiting a regular member of the congregation, there are certain expectations that have become the norm through the years. It may be a new experience for the parishioner to have the pastor visit, but there is still some idea of why the pastor has come. If the parishioner or the pastor is new to the congregation, there may need to be a little explaining about the role.

There are several things that are usually expected of pastors regardless of tradition: prayer and communion, for example. Anyone can come and pray, but the parishioners and families like the pastor to pray. Communion is something that not just anyone can do and still be in keeping with tradition. This sets the pastor apart in a special way, providing that which others cannot. How the pastor is addressed is sometimes a matter of tradition: Pastor, Father, Reverend, Minister, and even Preacher are common titles that are given to clergy. Tradition and culture also dictate rituals that the pastor may use when visiting: laying on of hands, kneeling to pray, anointing with oil, and sprinkling of holy water. Some parishioners are not so interested in what the pastor does as long as he or she takes off his or her coat and stays a while. Eating with the family is an expectation of some families. It may be helpful at times for the pastor to ask, rather than assume, what needs to be done. A simple question like, "So what do we need to do today?" will often gain for the pastor good insight as to the parishioner's expectation.

The role of pastor carries with it a measure of authority. I opened my office door one day to hear a commotion by the elevator. When I went to investigate, a psychiatric patient was slinging around three or four nurses, who were literally holding on for dear life. I recognized immediately that the nurses needed some assistance, and I walked over to the man. I looked at him and realized I needed all the power I could muster when I addressed him. I asked the nurses his name, realizing that calling him by name could gain for me his attention and also some power. They told me his name was Randy. I had no idea if he would be aware of what a chaplain was in a hospital, and I did not want to confuse him by calling myself a pastor when I was not standing in the door of a church. Also in the back of my mind was the thought: *There may only be one chance to pull this off, so I had to do it right.*

I spoke with as much authority as I could command in my voice, "Randy! This is Reverend Beverly." Just as I had hoped, he stopped what he was doing immediately and became as gentle as a lamb. I said to him, "These people are trying to take you back to the unit where you need to go so they can help you." I had gotten that information from one of the nurses. He asked me with the most timid demeanor, "Will you go with me?" I said I would, and I rode the elevator with him to the unit to which they were taking him. All of what we have talked about and many other dynamics are at play the moment that a person walks up and says, "My name is . . ."

Identity of the Other

The third point that we will consider is the name of the person to whom we are presenting ourselves. Just as we own our own name and have the right to decide what part of that name to share with someone else, the person with whom we are relating has that same prerogative. It is inappropriate for a pastor to learn the name of someone from some other source and address that person by that name without his or her permission. There have often been times when I have introduced myself to patients as Urias Beverly the chaplain, but they introduce themselves to me as Jones, Green, or Williams; and that was all that they gave me. I got the message immediately that as far as they were concerned this relationship was going to be based on the highest level of respect for them as people. As patients in the hospital they had lost their familiar surroundings, their daily schedule, their accustomed diet, their television programming, their privacy, and often functions of their body. The one thing they had left was a sense of pride, which they were not about to give away, not even to a chaplain. It is important that a pastor respect the boundary that they set by the name that they choose to give to him or her.

My father spent the last years of his life in two different nursing homes. In the first nursing home, the staff referred to him as Roy, something not even his late wife had used in relating with him. They had simply taken it off of the chart and felt for some reason it was all right to call a ninety-one-year-old man by his first name. My dad was a pastor and continued to pastor a church even while in the nursing home. To my knowledge no one had ever called him anything but Reverend R. W. Beverly for as long as I could remember. He said to me one day at the first nursing home, "If you don't get me out of this place, I'm going to just leave." I moved him to another nursing home where people referred to him as Reverend Beverly. He was very happy there and became the resident chaplain of the nursing home. It is always best to use the name people give you in relationship.

Some people are accustomed to a nickname or a name that they use with friends and family. If they are never allowed to share their name, the pastor may never know about this and never hear the parishioner say, "I like for my friends to call me by a certain name." It's a positive sign that the relationship is getting off to a good start. It is just as significant that parishioners have the opportunity to share their own names and set their own boundaries as it is for the pastor to share his or her name. What's in a name? A lot!

2. Establishing Rapport

It is so important that pastors take time to put the person they are ministering to at ease. Even if it is someone they have known for a long time, it is helpful to spend a moment helping him or her relax in the moment of his or her difficult situation. Here are several helpful suggestions:

Setting Parameters
Once a level of comfort has been established, the parameters of the relationship may be further defined. The role identification of pastor, chaplain, therapist, reverend or whatever title is given, begins to set the parameters for the relationship. The next step in the process is to help the person who is being aided become more comfortable with the process. The level of comfort in the process is highly correlated with the level of trust. It is difficult for persons to trust other persons that they do not know. Perhaps this is even truer when the person does not know the rules of this relationship and/or the boundaries thereof. The first thing the pastor needs to do at this point is to acquaint the parishioner with the purpose of this visit. Many patients in the hospital believe the chaplain only visits when someone is going to die. Some parishioners believe the only time the pastor wants to talk to them is when they have done something wrong or when money is needed. Knowing the nature of the encounter helps establish rapport and puts the parishioner at ease.

In the case where the individual has come to the office of the pastor, it is very important for the pastor to put that person at ease in his or her office. I often joke with students and clients who come to my office by saying to them I am aware that this is a new situation for them and it's normal for them to be anxious, but I have a rule in my office that people can only be anxious for five minutes, after which they must calm down and be relaxed. For those of you who understand the counseling lingo, it's paradoxical intention I use to help put people at ease. I also ask them about the difficulty they had finding the place since there are often problems finding a place the first time; this gives me an opportunity to empathize with the feeling that people often have when their anxiety causes them to have trouble finding a place that would otherwise not be a problem. It also gives me a chance to compliment them when they say they had no problem at all. It is good to begin with a compliment.

Commonality

The next thing the pastor may want to do is to identify areas that she or he has in common with the parishioner. At the same time, the pastor wants to be certain that these commonalities are subjects of interest to the parishioner. For example, the pastor may ask a man, or a woman as well, "Do you like sports?" If this is an area of interest to the parishioner, the pastor can follow up "With what kind of sport?" After that the questions continue to become more specific. If you are talking to a mother, it is often easy to develop some commonalities around children. If she happens to be a grandmother, grandchildren might be a good starting point. A pastor may usually safely assume that a mother or grandmother will enjoy talking about her grandchildren and will have pictures of them. Others things that the pastor may have in common with parishioners include music, art, traveling, movies, foods, and hobbies. I intentionally have not included religious affiliation. It certainly is not inappropriate, however, for that subject to come up and be explored, *if* it is raised by the parishioner.

Sometimes even questions raised about simple things will stimulate stories that the parishioner needs and wants to tell. One must remember that this phase of the relationship is establishing rapport, which means making the parishioner comfortable and building trust. It is essential to be patient and to listen with interest as the person begins to allow the pastor to come to know him or her. Once the trust level has reached a point that the parishioner is comfortable and is willing to share openly, it suggests that the relationship can move to the next phase. These phases are not rigidly divided and there is no reason why the pastor and/or the parishioner cannot move comfortably back and forth between phases. However, in most cases it is necessary to establish rapport before one can expect to move to the next stage of gathering background information.

3. Gathering Background Information

Confidentiality

Let's now discuss the issue of confidentiality. It is very important that people understand, even before they begin to give information to the pastor, how that information will be used and who will have access to it. It is important to be honest in this regard. Students sometimes must share that they may have to report this information to their supervisor or talk about it in a group. It's important that they assure the person who is giving the information that their identity will be protected. The pastor should be acquainted with the laws in the state in which he or she is pastoring. There are some things that cannot be held in strict confidence and the pastor should know that and be able to communicate that to the parishioner, particularly if the parishioner raises an issue about confidentiality. The pastor must be careful not to get boxed into a situation that is life-threatening and have no place to go without breaking his or her word. Most states will require the pastor to report to the appropriate authorities information regarding suicide, homicide, and/or abuse of children or elderly persons. One would not want to make such a big issue of confidentiality at this point as to divert the attention of the parishioner away from the relationship that is trying to be established. When rapport is established and trust is at a good level, it is time to get to work.

Basic Information

Now that the way is paved for the parishioner to share in great depth, the pastor can begin to ask for information about the parishioner that *will enhance the comfort level of the person*. These questions are mostly demographic kinds of questions related to marriage, children, birthplace, and work. This list of questions is for the sake of getting to know a person and is not in any particular order. There are several things that the pastor may keep in mind however; the intent of this part of the process is still to establish a relationship. If the pastor asks questions that raise the parishioner's anxiety, it will have the opposite effect of establishing rapport and cause the person to move away from relationship. A question like "Are you married?" particularly in this day and age where divorce is so common and people subscribe to many different lifestyles other that of marriage, may raise one's defenses to a point that rapport would be difficult, if at all possible, to establish.

One rule of thumb that may be helpful at this point of the process is to ask questions that are more distant from the person in time and/or space. The further away the information is from where the person is at present, the more comfortable the person may be in responding to the question. For example, a question of "Where are you from?" is much less threatening than the question "Where do you live?" "What is your occupation?" may be a better question than "Where do you work?" and certainly better than "Are you employed?" "Do you have family?" could replace "Are you married?"

While these questions seem to be, and are, requesting the same information, the subtle difference in the way they are worded gives the other person the opportunity to answer in a way that may be less embarrassing, less intrusive, and less direct. Take the question "Do you have family?" for example. Such a question allows the person to identify his and her own family and does not imply to them that marriage is something that they should have achieved by now. It's also a question that opens up the possibility for more information than just marital status. So it's a question that the pastor gets more mileage out of because it offers the opportunity for the parishioner to talk about spouse, children, parents, siblings, friends, partners, relatives, and household pets. Some people even include their church members as part of their family.

The question "Where are you from?" is more distant than "Where do you live?" It is at least more distant in time and often more distant in space. The word *family* is certainly more distant than the word *marriage*. It is much easier for people to talk about what happened when and where when it is some distance away from here and now. I often say to students that you want to ask questions that are far away in space and time as though you were focusing with a high-powered telescope lens. Gradually you bring the questions in closer until you are actually in the here and now. With each question, more trust is being established, and, consequently, responding to more threatening questions becomes easier.

Personal Information

A question that is often in the mind of the pastor is "What should I share as a pastor with the parishioner?" The rule of thumb I use for sharing personal information with the parishioner is that two criteria must be satisfied: (1) the person must request the information, and (2) the information must contribute to establishing rapport. Sometimes it is very difficult not to volunteer information. Fox example, if you ask a parishioner where he or she is from and they answer from a city where you have spent time, it is very difficult not to blurt out, "I spent ten years in that city." With a little patience and facial expression, the pastor can often generate a question from the parishioner, "Have you ever been there?" Or "Do you know where that is?" Or "I'll bet you've never heard of that place." If the pastor is genuinely interested in gathering information about the parishioner and establishing rapport, the person in most cases has the same interest and goal at heart. Rapport comes almost instantly when a person realizes that the pastor has lived in the same place he or she has lived. Even if you have not lived there, if you have been to it, passed through it, or came near it, the effect is the same for the parishioner. I have even asked for directions and said that I must look for it the next time I am out that way, and the parishioner felt at home with me.

Importance of Background Information

Enough cannot be said about gathering background information. It is at this stage of the process that the pastor can begin moving toward a spiritual diagnosis. The more information the pastor has, the better he or she can understand what needs to happen next. Without proper information he or she is walking in the dark. One would not appreciate a doctor writing a prescription without gaining all of the patient's health history. A pastor needs the history of the person with whom he or she is working before steps toward a remedy can be taken.

As the pastor moves to gathering background information, the relationship is very important. If it is not strong enough, the person may not feel comfortable sharing all that the pastor needs to know. If the conversation gets to a point where the person stops and is afraid to answer or share any more, the pastor needs to go back to building rapport and do some work. This may happen several times in an interview, but it is well worth the effort if the pastor wants to see the whole picture.

One thing that the pastor must accept is that the parishioner may not tell everything in the first visit, regardless of the effort to establish a relationship. This is the parishioner's right and responsibility; the pastor must respect that. The flip side of this issue is the parishioner that wants to tell it all with no regard to discretion. Often after a person does this, he or she may feel embarrassed later, which may lead to guilt, anger, shame, or fear. He or she may feel he or she told too much. It is not unusual that the parishioner will blame the pastor for pulling the information out of him or her, even though the information was shared freely. Although the pastor may not be to blame for such a situation, he or she does have some responsibility to help preserve the parishioner's dignity, especially in a crisis situation. An alert pastor will notice when the parishioner begins to share sensitive information and may stop the process and assure the person that he or she does not need to go on at that level of sharing unless it is helpful for him or her to do so. As the pastor hears the story of the parishioner, he or she begins to analyze what is being heard so at some point he or she can draw conclusions about the whole matter.

4. Spiritual Diagnosis and Treatment

Once the pastor has gathered the background information, a diagnosis can be made. The process of diagnosis begins when the interview begins. Everything that is said or not said, and done or not done is a piece of the puzzle. A wise pastor is always listening and looking for pieces that help to make sense of the situation. When the pastor tries to make a diagnosis and finds something is missing, he or she may need to ask questions that will help fill in or clear up data. Remember a proper diagnosis cannot be made without all of the information.

How does one make a spiritual diagnosis? A spiritual diagnosis includes body, mind, and spirit. It takes into account social, psychological, physical, mental, and cultural data. The equipment for this process is good common sense, experience, intuition, logic, rational thinking, theological understanding, and the Holy Spirit. The diagnosis may include how one understands the information he or she has given. Often the person has drawn what seems to him or her to be the only possible conclusion to a matter. The pastor may recognize immediately that there are other conclusions that may be just as valid. The diagnosis includes the notion that this person may be given to interpreting experience in a certain way or has a narrow perspective on events that occur.

Spiritual issues have to do with *connectedness*. How is one connected to himself, others, the environment, nature, and God? How does this person feel about himself or herself? How does he or she feel about life? What is the person's assessment about the situation at hand? Does his or her assessment make sense rationally? How open is the person to working through the issues? What does this person see as a solution to the problem? Where does God or religion fit into this entire matter? Does this person feel alienated from God? Does he or she seem to feel anger, guilt, shame, remorse, hopelessness, despair, and so forth? Does it seem that this person can make good use of a pastor? These are some of the questions that run through the mind of the pastor during the diagnostic phase.

Needless to say, a pastor may not be able to answer all of these questions after one interview; nor does every question need to be answered in every case. Some of the answers can only come as a result of the ongoing pastoral relationship. This relationship includes active listening (a process of feeding back to the speaker what is being heard so he or she can affirm what you are hearing or correct your assumptions), being supportive both verbally and nonverbally, clarifying perceptions and confronting false and/or irrational fears and assumptions, and being nonjudgmental. How the person responds becomes part of the diagnosis. The last part of the diagnosis is to determine what needs to happen next. This leads directly into the final phase of developing a relationship, which is closing.

5. Closing

The last phase, the closing, has several steps: (a) summary, (b) comforting/reappointment, and (c) benediction. One way to look at an interview with a parishioner in relation with a pastor is like how one might look at a surgery. Indeed, to the person going through this process it may feel like surgery. In the surgery, the patient is gradually prepared and made comfortable—put to sleep. An incision is made and things are moved around. Some things may be repaired, others may be removed. Yet some are assessed to be fine just as they are. When the parishioner tells his or her story and answers the pastor's questions, the intervention of the pastor may move some things around, help the person vent some things out, repair other things by reframing, and affirming things that are healthy. Now it is time to close the incision.

Summary

In closing one must be careful to put everything back. Take out all foreign items that do not belong there and sew everything back together in a neat and healthy fashion. This is what the summary does: It helps to pull together all that has happened in the interview. The most ideal summary is to have the parishioner do it alone. The pastor may ask, "What have we covered in our conversation today?" If the parishioner can list the subjects that have been discussed, it is probably an unusual parishioner, although many will remember some of the issues. The next most ideal summary is the pastor and parishioner together. He or she will ask the same questions as above, and if there is little or no response, he or she will list one or two subjects and wait for the parishioner to add to the list. Then the pastor will list one or two more and wait again. If this fails, the pastor will have to move to plan three in which he or she will list slowly each subject covered, encouraging agreement of each from the parishioner. When the summary is complete, the incision has been closed and the pastor can move on toward comforting.

Comforting/Reappointment

Continuing with the metaphor of surgery, comforting is like protecting the wound with a bandage, giving a prescription for pain, setting another appointment, and conveying availability. The pastor asks how the parishioner is feeling, affirms the parishioner for doing good work, shows appreciation for being trusted, and gives words of hope and encouragement. The pastor then explores when they may talk together again. It is very important to understand that an appointment is like a sacred trust. The relationship may be destroyed if the pastor fails to keep an appointment. It is better to be tentative about the next meeting until you can be sure of the exact time than to plan an exact time and not make it.

The appointment should be realistic in terms of the pastor's time and energy and also reflect the seriousness of the situation. A crisis situation may require another appointment in twenty-four to forty-eight hours rather than a week later. Where the meeting should take place may need to be considered. It may also be important to include other people in the meeting and/or to have certain tasks accomplished before the meeting takes place. These tasks may need to be completed by the parishioner, the pastor, or both. The appointment grows out of the pastor's diagnosis and is part of the pastor's suggested treatment plan.

The tasks may be a prescription given to the parishioner by the pastor to help manage the pain as it were. I often will insist that people eat, rest, recreate, get some questions answered, attend church services, move away from an unsafe place, read or write something, or have a complete medical checkup. When I prescribe these things I often tell them not to come back without having done it. Sometimes I do not set another appointment until they call and tell me they have done what I requested. The tasks often give the parishioner a sense of control in the situation; there is something they can do. It also helps them realize that it is their problem and they are the ones who must solve it, not the pastor. The *midwife* cannot have the baby for the mother.

After the prescription is given, I then give the person the information and the permission to contact me if necessary. This is like putting on a bandage. I have seen how people in crisis have held on to my business card when I tell them it makes me available to them all of the time, even at home (be careful about giving out your home number). If I want the person to trust me, I have to trust the person too. I tell them they must not share the information with anyone else and they must promise me that they will call me if they get into crisis again. Only one person has ever called me at home, but many have at the hospital. Sometimes I believe they are just checking to see if it really works. Jesus said, "I will send you a comforter" (John 16:7 paraphrased). The availability of the pastor to the parishioner is very comforting indeed.

Benediction

The benediction is the blessing that comes just before departing. It may include prayer, silence, scripture, song, words of comfort, reassurance, hugging, handshake, or touching. These are powerful tools and should not be used indiscriminatively. It is not wise to expect most people to refuse any of these blessings if the pastor were to ask. Yet they should only be used when the parishioner is ready and willing. The pastor may ask if there is anything the parishioner would like before they end their time together. This allows the parishioner the freedom to express his or her desire or lack thereof. If the pastor needs to pray, for example, to feel more comfortable himself or herself, he or she should not try to pretend it is for the benefit of the parishioner. He or she should say, "I have a need to pray, is that all right?"

Touch is something that should happen only after much discernment. Even then it is most important to touch appropriately. Sometimes the parishioner will want to be touched or hugged and then feel bad about it later. The other reaction may be that the parishioner wants more hugging and touching in the future. These tools are so powerful, especially in the hands of a pastor, that they must not ever be used unadvisedly. No one outside of the relationship can say when touching is appropriate, but one should be careful in determining for oneself. A rule of thumb for touching or any other pastoral tool is, "For whose benefit am I using this tool?" If the pastor is honest and knows it is to make him or herself feel better, it is a good sign that using the tool is inappropriate. Even language that is used in the tender, intimate moment can be dangerous. While I have urged caution, I also urge healing and blessing. The parishioner needs a pastor and tools of a pastor bring healing. May I refer to what I said earlier: "A good relationship covers a multitude of sins." So don't be afraid to show concern, caring, compassion, and comfort; but be sure to do it in the context of judicious discernment.

HEALING THROUGH RELATIONSHIP

People often come to the pastor because they do not feel whole in some way. Whatever the circumstances, the root of the problem is the person's inability "to establish and maintain mutually need-satisfying relationships."[6] "We human beings are open systems. Our growth takes place in relationships. . . . Pastoral care and counseling are effective to the extent that they help persons increase their ability to relate in ways that nurture wholeness in themselves and others."[7] The most helpful way to begin to help someone who has difficulty in relationships is for the pastor to establish and maintain a relationship with the person, as arduous as that might be. Some people believe they cannot have a satisfying relationship with any other human being; the pastor can show them that it can happen. Once they experience a satisfying relationship with the pastor, hopefully they can then extrapolate that experience to others.

Once a good relationship is established, it can be used to resolve the problem. Howard Clinebell says, "Counseling consists of the establishment and subsequent utilization of a relationship. . . . Counseling techniques are helpful only within such a context."[8] "Instead of worrying about what one is going to say or do next . . . , the counselor should focus energy on being aware of and with the person in an alive human relationship."[9] Even if the pastor is highly skilled and has extensive training, the best techniques in the world still cannot take the place of or be as effective as a good pastoral relationship.

Some books that focus on relational techniques put too much pressure on the pastor to know what to say or do to bring about wholeness and healing in the parishioner. Even when a technique has worked in many other situations, every situation and person is different and the same technique may not be effective *this* time. And sometimes you only have one chance. Tending to the relationship first, no matter how difficult, always improves the chances that a technique will be effective, but be aware that when a person is in trouble he or she may be afraid, anxious, confused, or just not know what the real issues are and therefore send strange signals. Even a very intuitive person will be confused at what he or she is hearing and seeing.

THE LIMITS OF THE PASTORAL RELATIONSHIP

Parish pastors are well advised to limit their counseling of parishioners to short-term (three to six sessions) dealing with responses to recent situations. This counseling contrasts with professional pastoral counseling, which is characterized by long-term care (formal, structured, weekly sessions) dealing with issues that often have been a problem for a long time. In any case, the counseling process begins and continues with an authentic relationship between the pastor and the parishioner(s). All tech-niques of pastoral care and counseling, no matter who is doing the counseling, are authenticated, justified, and made more effec-tive by the quality of the relationship between the pastor and the parishioner. It doesn't matter how long the pastor has had a rela-tionship with a parishioner; when the time comes for special help, that relationship needs to be deepened and strengthened to bear the weight of the new situation.

Although it is God who does the healing and transforming in all contexts, the pastor can be either a facilitator or an obstacle to God's work. The pastor must be willing to get involved with the parishioner. Pastors are the midwives and/or bridges of healing and comfort. A mother brought her son to the pastor to talk to him about cutting class at school and getting into trouble. The teenager spoke only in slang and vulgar language. The pastor reminded him of where he was (in God's house) and with whom he was speaking; he must be respectful. The young man shared very little after that. The pastor asked a schoolteacher in his congregation, "How do you get through to these boys with all of their language and all?" The teacher responded, "I don't know about you, pastor, being a man of the cloth and all, but sometimes I have to get right down with them and use some language they understand." The next Sunday the pastor saw the teen and spoke briefly to him, "I want you to come back and see me; I believe God can overlook our language until we work through this problem." The teen smiled and said, "Catch you later, Rev." This was the beginning of a good and productive relationship. Since relationship is key to pastoring, let's talk some about how to develop it and sustain it.

PASTORAL IDENTITY—CALLED TO LOVE AS GOD LOVES

When people feel secure and safe enough to share their life his-tory, painful stories pour forth as blood from a picture of gloom, with all the agony of physical, emotional, and sexual abuse—often at the hands of their flesh and blood parents and family members. Horror stories of rape and robbery, sexism and racism, deception and betrayal, and worse things are shared by people who are emotionally wounded, physically and mentally scared, spiritually broken, angry at the world, and lacking in self-esteem. These are the stories of the past, which leave the victims to waste away in despair or find a way to cope and live again.

Currently, we are experiencing terrorist attacks, massive layoffs, crime in the streets, drug houses in the neighborhoods, and the swindling of employees' life savings by the company for which they work and the executives that they trusted. Besides all of this are the regular hurricanes, tornadoes, floods, fires, earthquakes, volcanoes erupting, explosions and airplane crashes.

The tragedies mentioned above and many others leave people in the most devastating psychological and spiritual condition that we could ever have imagined. It would appear that a large, evil vacuum has engulfed and consumed our society. Many have fallen into this vacuum of horror, which the Scriptures characterize as trouble and discomfort; some have felt the deliverance from these troubles by the hand of almighty God. Sometimes only a merciful God can comfort the grief and pain that is left in the wake of awful calamities of this life. Out of the pool of the divinely rescued, God calls women and men into ministry. As pastors, they "have been comforted in their troubles, by the God of all compassion, so they can comfort others in any trouble" (2 Cor. 1:4). This is the foundation of a pastor's identity; he or she is called by God to love as God loves.

Who Am I?

If I am a man or a woman who has received God's comfort, mercy, and blessing in my own troubles, I know what it means to have troubles; but most of all, I know what it means to be rescued by God and comforted by God's grace during times of trouble. I may or may not be ordained; I may be old or young, rich or poor, educated or not. The one thing that separates me from anybody else is that I feel called in one way or another, through my experience, by some apparition, dream, and so forth, to help comfort others in their troubles. It started as a small thing for me to just help someone who was having some difficulty, but it grew, and it now consumes me. I find myself seeking opportunities to help people and wanting to learn all that I can about how to be more effective in helping.

Whose Am I?

Many times it is a thankless job that I do, but my fulfillment comes in knowing who I am and whose I am. My life is no longer my own and does not consist of doing what pleases me; it belongs to the One who has called me, and my joy is in doing what I believe God wants me to do. Of all the other things I have done in my life, this feels more like what I am cut out for and meant to be and do than anything else I have ever done. I would never have chosen this path of work for myself; I hardly feel that I am capable or worthy to do it. Yet I am not able to help myself. When someone in need calls upon me, I know I must respond. Even if I do not feel that I am able to help, I must try and depend on God to make things come out right.

The Call to Ministry

The call to ministry is not something that happens once and for all; it is a continuous process of calling and calling again. The call is related to the capacity of the minister to be with troubled persons in a meaningful way. Contrary to what ministers often feel, God seems to only lay on us those things that we are able to do with God's help. This dimension of the call suggests that we are not only called to minister to particular people. As our competence increases so does the field of our ministry. This raises the question of, "Who are those that I am called to serve?" The answer is, all of those who need help.

Who Are We?

Simply put, we are the church no matter where we go, no matter the context or setting. As pastors, we are called to comfort others with the comfort we continually receive from God. The only way we can accomplish this is through power of a relationship. A relationship is a connection with and to another person or persons. If we are to pass on to the other the comfort we have received form God, we must be connected; that is, we must have strong relationships with God and others. This is like a blood transfusion: there must be a connection to convey the blood from one person to the other person. It is our responsibility to connect ourselves to those in trouble and become their comfort, just as God comforts us.

Now that we have looked at the basics of building a relationship, we will look at the importance of the setting. In each setting establishing rapport is a little different as is the pastor's role and authority. Each setting has particular rituals, etiquette, and dilemmas for the pastoral relationship. Each subsequent chapter will focus on these topics and helpful resources for your ministry.

NOTES

1. W. E. Vine, *An Expository Dictionary of New Testament Words* (Nashville: Thomas Nelson Publishing, 1952), p. 839.

2. Ibid.

3. Ibid., p. 53.

4. Ibid., p. 54.

5. Rodney Hunter, ed., *Dictionary of Pastoral Care and Counseling* (Nashville: Abingdon Press, 1990), p. 850.

6. Howard Clinebell, *Basic Types of Pastoral Counseling* (New York: Abingdon Press, 1966), p. 28.

7. Ibid., p. 31.

8. Ibid., p. 74.

9. Ibid., p. 75.

TWO

IN THE
PARISHIONER'S
HOME

Before the Second World War it was very common for pastors to visit parishioners in their homes. As large hospitals were built, people with ailments were moved into those facilities (mostly for the convenience of doctors and ancillary medical people) and pastors began to visit more at the hospitals. Later, as nursing homes became more and more plentiful, the elderly were institutionalized there and pastors made their visits at nursing homes. As church buildings began to be built and/or remodeled, they offered pastors offices in which to meet with families to discuss matters like weddings, baptisms, and funerals. It was easier for the pastors because they had all the resources at hand. Visits to the pastor's office became increasingly popular because many families lived some distance from their church.

Parishioners contributed to this dynamic as well; many of them did not want the pastor to visit them in their home. There were several reasons for this: they did not want the pastor to see where they lived or how they lived; they did not want or have the time to clean the house; they could not get the family together long enough for a pastoral visit; and the fast-moving pace of society did not allow anyone in the household time to cook, which many felt was expected if the pastor was visiting.

But home visits are becoming popular again for at least two reasons: (1) the hospice movement, which has moved people from the institution back into their own homes to die, and (2) with Medicaid, Medicare, and insurance companies paying less and less for medical procedures, hospitals are releasing people earlier and earlier. This means that the patients must go home to recover, rather than recuperate in the hospital as they used to. So more and more pastors find themselves making home visits again.

There are a couple of additional reasons for home visits: many parishioners, especially older people, still harbor the expectation that the pastor should visit them in their home; and some parishioners want the pastor to visit to encourage their nonattending family members to attend church. In addition, many pastors see visitation in the home as a means to extend the church's invitation and hospitality to people who have visited, but not joined, their church. This being the case, it is important that we look at effective ways to visit parishioners in their homes.

ESTABLISHING RAPPORT

In the previous chapter, we spoke at length about establishing a pastoral relationship. The basic concept is the same, whether it is visiting people in the institution or in their homes. There is one overriding factor, however, that must be noted when visiting patients in their home: *it is their* space. Many people have an idea how they would like to entertain in their own space and the best way to establish rapport is to let them do it their own way. My wife, Billie, who is also a pastor, and I visited one of my parishioners who is more than ninety years old. She lives alone and is very alert and in charge. She was extremely glad to see us when we came with our seven-year-old granddaughter. She invited us in, gave each of us a hug, and encouraged us to sit down. She had a special seat for each one of us. It was a cool day, and my seat was too close to the register. In a gracious act she insisted that I move it away because in a little while I would be too warm. Once she had all of us in place where she wanted us, she pulled up her own rocker, which she said she reserved for company.

She has an ironclad memory and is well-versed on everything that is going on. In fact, she had told the woman at church who sends bulletins to the sick and shut-in that sending her a bulletin did not do her any good. Tell her some of what was going on, she requested. The church member complied, and she has gotten information about what's happening at church on a regular basis ever since. She also told us about one of the church members who visited her and was looking for a particular crest of his school. She had one of her great-nieces, a computer whiz, find the crest and send him a picture of it. She told us all about her family and about the history of her involvement at the church. She kept saying she was talking too much and was probably boring us, but she didn't stop.

When we finally said that we had to leave, she offered no resistance, whereupon we stood, joined hands together, and my wife prayed a prayer for all of us. At the end of my wife's prayer, our parishioner began praying another prayer for all of us. It was a very good prayer, but of course it was in her own style. Once we were in the car, my wife realized because we had been there so long, she would not be able to visit two other people. This is not to take away from the joy and fulfillment of visiting with this woman, but only to point out that when visiting in someone's home, the pastor is on the other person's turf and must allow him or her the freedom to set the agenda. To resist the efforts of the parishioner to conduct a visit in the way he or she sees fit would be to resist establishing the level of rapport that makes for a good relationship and effective pastoral care. By the way, we took our granddaughter with us not necessarily for the purpose of establishing rapport, but her presence certainly gave our parishioner permission to talk about her own family and great-great-grandchildren, although she really did not need it.

PASTOR'S ROLE

Regardless of where the pastor is meeting, whether in the home of the parishioner, in the pastor's office, or someplace else, the pastor has a distinct role. Recently I attended an appreciation program for a pastor of long-standing in a church. A parishioner made this comment, "If you need him at the hospital when you are going into surgery, he is there early in the morning. Not only is he there, but he is there in a three-piece suit." In her affirmation and compliment of her pastor, this woman was stating an expectation of her pastor's role. She was saying, in effect, that part of what I expect from my pastor is that he dress professionally when he is doing pastoral care. Although part of this woman's expectation may have been cultural, in a broader sense pastors must be mindful of the role they play in the lives of parishioners.

Even when a pastor and a parishioner are close friends, the parishioner may still expect the pastor to be "pastoral" in their relationship. In many cases the friendship has developed because of the pastoral dimension of the relationship. Although the role of the pastor will vary from tradition to tradition and parishioner to parishioner, whatever that established role is the pastor must be aware of it when visiting in the parishioner's home. My own feeling is that whatever is expected of the pastor at the church is expected even more in the parishioner's home.

When Jesus went to a dinner at Simon's house, a woman came in and began to cry over his feet and dry her tears with her hair (Luke 7). Simon said to himself: "This man must not really be a prophet because if he were, he would know what kind of woman this is." While we understand such comments served several different purposes, it is important to look at the role expectation that was implicit in this comment. What the detractors were trying to say was that Jesus had a public reputation as a prophet. He had demonstrated his claim to this role on several occasions. Even those that were against him and his ministry could not take away from the way he executed his prophetic responsibilities. However, in the privacy of Simon's home, they felt that he had relaxed his standards and allowed himself to be taken in by someone of ill repute. The pastor does not want to behave rigidly or piously in a parishioner's home, but certainly the pastor must be aware that he or she has a role and a standard of behavior that is expected in the home of the parishioner.

In a parishioner's home, pastors are often invited to relax, let their hair down, and be themselves. To the parishioner this may mean off-color jokes, drinking, smoking, playing cards, or just plain old gossiping. The idea is that they want the pastor to be comfortable in their home. This may well be the case, but whatever a pastor does at one parishioner's house is sure to find its way to the entire congregation in time. Be sure that you do nothing that you would not like publicized on Sunday morning. Another thing about joining in with parishioners in their style of fun is that they may like you more for joining in, but respect you less. The influence of pastors often lies not in how well they are liked, but how well they are respected. Let all pastors beware if they need to have fun; it is better to have their own friends with which to have fun than to depend on their own parishioners for having a good time.

PASTOR'S AUTHORITY

One of the most difficult things for pastors to learn to use well is their own personal and professional authority. Some pastors underuse their authority and get into trouble, because in the absence of their own authority someone else's authority becomes the order of the day. It is probably more frequent, however, that pastors misuse the power that is given to them.

When my friend Clinton McNair studied for his Ph.D. in Chicago, he had an unusual and powerful experience. He was majoring in pastoral counseling and was working part-time in a clinic. This clinic provided counseling for people who were poor and marginalized in many ways. The problem arose that some of the counselees were not showing up for their sessions even though the counseling was free. A survey indicated that one of the prevalent problems was the lack of transportation, so a decision was made to experiment with doing pastoral counseling in people's homes.

Dr. McNair reported that when he showed up at the home of the counselees he had a startling experience: the families had cleaned the house, sent all of the neighborhood children home, turned off the television and the telephone, and called the family together in the living room. They were so honored to have the pastor in their home that they made every provision to entertain and to be available to the pastor. The level of respect and deference that was given to the pastor gave him a lot of authority. It is not uncommon that parishioners will receive the pastor in their home with this level of respect, honor, and deference. Although it feels good to have this much authority, a large responsibility accompanies it. The pastor must be careful to never do harm or abuse his or her authority in anyone's home.

How does a pastor maximize the benefit of having the authority given by parishioners and yet be careful not to misuse or abuse that authority? It is important for the pastor to remember that he or she is also under authority. In the scripture when Jesus was on his way to Jerusalem and asked his disciples to go ahead and find a place to spend the night, the Samaritans refused to house them. Two of his disciples suggested that they call down fire from heaven on those who refused them. They had just recently been given the power to cast out demons, but now the demons were in them. Jesus had to stop them, correct them, and chastise them because they had let their authority go to their heads and had forgotten their mission (Luke 9:51-56). The pastor must always be careful not to let authority go to his or her head. We as pastors are under authority. Our assignment is to care for those who need care without abuse, neglect, belittling, or taking over.

Pastors sometimes abuse their authority when they are asked to resolve issues in the home. As a rule of thumb, it is not a good thing to provide simple answers for complex problems. The answers need to be generated by those who are closest to the problem. The pastor's role is not to give the answers, but to empower those who are seeking the answers to find their own answers. It is one thing to give guidance and quite another thing to give answers. Even if the answers and/or recommendations work out well, it still defeats the greater good for parishioners because, now when they have a problem, they must call the pastor to solve it for them rather than find a solution on their own. It brings to mind the old axiom "Give someone a fish, you feed them; one day teach them how to fish, and you feed them for life." The pastor should use his or her authority to help parishioners claim their own authority and find their own solutions.

RITUAL AND ETIQUETTE

The pastor has no power in and of him or herself, but the rituals that pastors perform are very powerful. So it should surprise no one that during home visits some parishioners will take advantage of the opportunity to gain full benefit of the pastor's presence by asking for particular religious rituals. Other than communion or even baptism, you might be asked to perform other rituals. Since the pastor does not know what rituals he or she will be called upon to perform, it is important to have everything that may be needed. Such items that should be available to the pastor include a communion set, anointing oil, holy water, and a ritual book.

Blessing the Home

I am always honored when I am at someone's home and they say to me, "While you're here, Pastor, would you bless my house?" My purpose in visiting may have been to see a sick person, but the parishioner may feel that it may be a long time before I am there again. Sometimes it has been the desire of the parishioner for years to have their home blessed by the pastor. This ritual can be done a number of ways: providing readings and prayers in a stationary position, moving to each room of the home and pronouncing a blessing for each room, or using holy water (water that has been blessed by the use of special prayers) to sprinkle throughout the house with a blessing pronounced in each room.

Anointing the Sick with Oil

When you visit a home, in spite of how well you may know your parishioners, you will encounter people of different traditions, even within the full range of your own tradition. You might be surprised at what you will be asked to do. For example, it sometimes happens that someone in the home will expect that the sick person you are visiting needs to be anointed with oil. This is a biblical practice, but one that not all traditions honor; nevertheless, if you are asked, you should be clear in your mind how this anointing might take place.

When I as a kid got sick, my mother would rub my whole chest with some kind of oil to help me cough up whatever was bothering me. When I heard about anointing the sick with oil, this was my idea of what anointing was. I have since come to understand that anointing, as a ritual, is different from rubbing on oil as a treatment. Anointing as a ritual tends to focus on the head. One simple way of applying the oil is to the forehead. Aside from the oil that is used for the anointing ritual are the words that are used and the prayers that are said. It may be helpful to consult a ritual book to be prepared for this eventuality. However, the pastor should feel free to conduct this ritual in the style that is most helpful to the parishioner and most comfortable to the pastor.

Suppose the pastor happens to show up at the parishioner's home without a communion kit, anointing oil, or holy water. Does this mean that he or she must run back to the office and collect those items to be an effective pastor? Absolutely not! If the pastor has any power at all to perform rituals, the pastor also has the resources to create the substances necessary for the ritual.

What turns the communion elements into the proper host for communion? What makes the holy water holy? What makes anointing oil appropriate for anointing the sick? In spite of the fact that you could have these substances sent from a long distance away, and they would come with certain guarantees of effectiveness, the truth is that the parishioner will generally have what you need.

The same way you can say a blessing over these items at the church or any place else, you can also do in the parishioner's home with whatever substances are available, and it will have the same efficacy as any substance that you bring with you. If your problem is saying the right words, just be sure in your prayer to God to make the substance over which you are praying appropriate for whatever you are using it. Remember whatever ritual you are performing, the benefit of the ritual is the grace of God working through the ritual. It is not so much the words you say or the substance you use as it is the appeal to God to be present and make happen what needs to happen in that situation. Always remember, "I have planted, Apollos watered; but God gave the increase" (1 Cor. 3:6 KJV).

Manners

The first rule of etiquette for pastors at all times is to be kind, pleasant, and polite. Always remember that you are a guest in someone's home. As a guest you will be there for a relatively short period of time and then you will leave (an obvious but significant fact). Regardless of why you have been invited to this home, it is not proper to criticize the way people live. This means that he or she may live there any way he or she chooses to live. The pastor who enters a home with a judgmental attitude is a cantankerous guest. As the host has suspended his or her normal activities to be available to the guest, the guest must suspend his or her personal taste and idiosyncrasies to be of service to the host. Don't be fooled by the request of the host to offer your opinion on something in the home. As my father used to say, "If you can't say something good, do not say anything at all."

Eating and Drinking in the Parishioner's Home

It is very difficult, if not impossible, to visit someone's home and not have to deal with the issue of eating. In the old days, the rule was that the pastor must eat anything and everything that was offered to him or her. It was an insult not to accept whatever the parishioner had prepared in the home. I have heard elderly pastors complain about all the unwanted stuff they had to eat. Today, that rule does not apply nearly as strongly as it used to; however, many parishioners at least hope that the pastor will share bread when he or she comes to the house. There are some polite ways to refuse what is offered and not offend the parishioner. Some of the appropriate refusals are as follows: health, diet, and special plans such as a family birthday. It is a good thing for the pastor to have some rules that he or she lives by when he or she goes to people's houses. It is most important that these rules are observed by the pastor consistently. Word will get around very quickly that the pastor ate at one house but not at another.

Different traditions and cultures handle the question of alcohol differently. It is only good common sense for the pastor to not allow himself or herself to be seduced into participating in social drinking at a parishioner's house, especially if the pastor is driving. There may be a rare occasion in which a toast of wine may be appropriate, but beyond this, the pastor should be wise enough to refuse using a pastoral visit for an occasion of socializing in this way. Of course, if alcohol is detrimental to the pastor's health, the pastor must refuse. It is often detrimental to the pastor's professional health. Just as the pastor has to accept the boundaries that others set for themselves, parishioners must accept boundaries that pastors set for themselves. Again, it is important that the pastor be consistent about his or her boundaries, wherever the pastor may happen to be.

DILEMMAS

There are many dangerous pitfalls in visiting parishioners in their homes. I will address three of them at this time: sexual misconduct, spousal jealousy, and confidentiality. As you can see, all of these pitfalls are to some degree related, but I will address each one individually.

Sexual Misconduct

If there ever was any professional innocence in our society, it does not exist anymore. There are now several specialties of law related to pastoral sexual misconduct. Whenever anything of a sexual nature happens between a parishioner and a pastor, regardless of the behavior of the parishioner, it is generally accepted that the pastor is responsible, because the pastor is the professional and has a position of relative power. This means that the pastor is responsible if *any* sexual impropriety occurs, *no matter who initiated the behavior.* The pastor is the professional, the trained person, the experienced person, the one who is looked up to, and the one who has been given authority. It is the pastor's responsibility to make sure that the parishioner is safe, proper distance is maintained, and that all appropriate boundaries are maintained.

My personal feeling is that most pastors do not set out to do anything sexually inappropriate with a parishioner. I believe what generally happens is that pastors get caught in situations that they are not prepared to handle, and they make some grave mistakes on the spur of the moment that they would not make if they had time to reflect. It is too late to reflect in the middle of a situation. Pastors must have these issues resolved within themselves before they come in contact with the parishioner, or something could go wrong.

To explain this a little more, there is a psychological dynamic that is called *transference,* which is often at play between any two people in relationship. The term refers to the times when a parishioner associates a pastor with someone that the parishioner had a relationship with in the past. It could be a parent, sibling, friend, spouse, and so forth. When the parishioner associates the pastor with someone in the past, many of the feelings that the parishioner had for the person in the past or elsewhere at the moment are transferred to the pastor. If it is someone they loved, they then feel love for the pastor. Likewise, if they disliked the other person, they will dislike the pastor too.

The difficult thing about transference is that it is an unconscious process. People transferring feelings will likely not be aware of it; and when they are made aware of it, they cannot understand why they have such feelings. Men often marry women who have characteristics like their mothers. Women are attracted to men who are like their fathers. This is true (perhaps even more so) even if the man or woman does not like his or her parent. My wife is so much like my mother that it drives me nuts sometimes. I had no idea that I was replacing my mother when I got married. I tell my wife sometimes in no uncertain tones, "Don't call me like that! It sounds just like my mother."

I have worked on my personal feelings for my mother in therapy, so it is not the problem it once was. If I had not settled these mother issues and I was ministering to someone that reminded me of my mother, I would experience *countertransference*, the dynamic that can get ministers and other people-helpers in trouble. With the parishioner it is called *transference*; with the pastor (or other professional) it is *countertransference*. Transference in itself is not bad; in fact, it is often helpful to the process. It allows trust to exist where otherwise it would not. It gives authority to the pastor that otherwise may not happen. Sometimes it gives hope to the parishioner that may otherwise not be there. It allows a relationship to form and grow, which is necessary to address some issues.

Countertransference can be dangerous! It fools the pastor into thinking that he or she is the only one that can help a certain person. It allows pastors (men and women) to believe that true love has come between them and a parishioner. It lets the pastor believe all of the compliments that the parishioner gives. Countertransference can ease into the relationship and disorient the pastor's thinking and feeling until both the pastor and the parishioner are caught up into a web of secrecy and deceit. Once this happens, it is just a matter of time before both of them will find their lives ruined. The signs of countertransference are subtle but discernible. I once had a supervisor who defined transference as when a parishioner says to the pastor, "Pastor, you preached the best sermon today I have ever heard." He said countertransference is when the pastor believes it.

To avoid falling into this occupational hazard, pastors need to be sure that they have a satisfying relationship with a significant other, someone they can and do talk to about their day-to-day ministry. They should be careful if they find themselves extending the time they allotted to see someone. They should see parishioners in appropriate places and at appropriate times. Never (I seldom use that word) think of the parishioner as being on the same emotional and authority level as you are. Parishioners have years of experience looking up to pastors, and they are not about to undo all of that just because you are the pastor. The pastor is the stronger of the two, the one with the authority. It is your job to have your own stuff together, set appropriate boundaries for the relationship, and maintain them for both of you if necessary.

Pastors who do not have a healthy, intimate relationship with their spouse or significant other are much more likely to get caught up in sexual misconduct situations. Mind you, I did not say that pastors must be married or have a significant other; I said must have a healthy, intimate relationship. This means that if a pastor is having difficulties in his or her own marriage or relationship with his or her significant other, that pastor needs to be very, very careful as he or she makes visits to persons where sexual misconduct could occur.

Pastors who have a need to fix people and their problems are much more likely than other pastors to get caught up in sexual misconduct situations. If a pastor has a need to be needed and feels responsible for taking care of the needs of others, that pastor needs to take some extra precautions to avoid being a part of a sexual misconduct situation. A pastor named Jim (not his real name) was an easy-going guy. Sometimes people called him "good ol' Jim." He would say things like "Call me anytime." He meant it and would help anyone he could. He called me on two different occasions to help him help somebody. He was just a real nice guy. That was his problem: he was too nice. He never really believed that he was an effective minister, so he made up for it by helping everybody. Helping others made him feel good about himself.

Take it from me, for every one who needs to help others, there are others who need to be helped. Jim burned himself out taking on everybody's problems. He did not even see it when he lost his marriage, because he was always helping out somebody else. One night someone had a big fight with her husband and left the house, and she needed some special kind of help from Jim. She just wanted to be held and accepted as all right. Pastor Jim rushed to help and found, now that he no longer had his own loving relationship, that he had some needs of his own. They helped each other that night. Not long afterward, they helped each other again and again, each time going a little farther than the time before. In time, he lost the church and she lost her husband.

The greatest danger that a pastor faces in terms of sexual misconduct may be the pastor's own sense of self-confidence. Trust me when I tell you no matter how disciplined a pastor may be, no matter how noble a pastor's intentions are, no matter how filled with the Spirit or how fervent their prayers are, all pastors are human beings and thus susceptible to sexually embarrassing and damaging situations. Overconfidence is dangerous. Some pastors have a reputation for being Super Pastor. This is expressed in the fact that the pastor is the only one who can do the things that need to be done, even when the pastor is tired, sick, stressed, lonely, and so forth. This kind of pastor believes no one else can do it right and he or she must do it all.

Pastors should not overestimate themselves and their ability to perform at all times. Too much confidence will make a pastor believe he can be supportive of someone having marital problems right after having a big fight with his own spouse. Over-confidence will cause pastors to summit themselves to flattery and seduction, believing that it will never bother them. Over-confidence will lead some pastors to places they would never otherwise go.

I once had a client that was attracted to me. That was flattering enough in itself, considering she was very attractive, charming, and seductive. She used to suggest that we have our sessions somewhere else other than in my office. I was tempted, and I admitted it to myself and to her, but I told her, "See all of these certificates around my wall? I worked hard to get them, and now they are my friends; they remind me how difficult it was to get to where I am. So as long as I am in my office, I know what I will do and what I won't do. If I were to meet you somewhere else, I do not know what will happen. I am just too scared to take the chance, scared for you and scared for me." I have as much confidence as any man, more than most; but I am human, and I have to accept that, for my sake and for the parishioner.

What can we do? I am not one to require, as some liability insurance policies do, that a pastor never be with the opposite sex in a room alone with the door closed or that a pastor never touch a parishioner in any way at all. I am certainly not of the school that says a pastor must always have his or her spouse with him or her when visiting parishioners. And yet there may be good reasons that a pastor employs one or both of these restrictions. Regardless of whether or not a pastor takes someone along with him or her, there are some commonsense things that a pastor must do to avoid falling into one of these traps.

(1) **Visit at an appropriate time.** It is inappropriate to visit any parishioner early in the morning before the parishioner has had time to get out of bed and be fully dressed. This is asking for trouble. The same thing is true late at night. If there is a question that the parishioner may not be up, awake, and fully dressed, the pastor probably should not be visiting that home. The best thing to do is to call well in advance.

(2) **Keep your visits short and to the point.** The longer the visit goes on, the more chance there is for something to happen that was not supposed to happen. The same is true if the conversation wanders away from the intent of the visit. The pastor must exercise his or her authority to keep the conversation at least in the boundaries of the reason for the visit.

(3) Never visit anyone's home without telling someone where you are going. It should be understood by all of the parishioners that the pastor's spouse and/or the church secretary, among others, are always aware of where he or she is making a visit. These kinds of boundaries help pastors to avoid falling into temptation and breaking their vows, whether or not they intended to. It also reduces the occasions for secrecy.

As a pastoral counselor for many years and having visited in many people's homes, I have my own experience from which to draw. Not only have I visited people's homes as a pastor, but I also have been in many people's homes as a telephone repairman and handyman. I have had a lot of time in people's homes at various times of the day and night. I am still a firm believer that the best way to stay out of trouble in people's homes is to have a good relationship with them. A good relationship, as talked about in the first chapter of this book, allows the pastor to establish rapport and to maintain appropriate boundaries with people. In my experience, there have been very rare occasions that people urged me to cross a boundary that they knew I had set for myself and for them. Of course, there is some testing of the boundaries and a desire to know if the pastor is serious about the boundaries. But a pastor has a right to have his or her boundaries respected by the parishioner and to leave the home if those boundaries are compromised. Most people do not like to experience rejection. If they know that the answer to the question is no, they will be much less likely to ask the question than they would if they were not sure what the answer would be. My concluding statement on this matter is simply a quote from the Scriptures: "Be wise as serpents and harmless as doves" (Matt. 10:16 NKJV).

This topic is of such serious concern that most denominations have guidelines and training about sexual misconduct. Take advantage of all the training you can get.

Spousal Jealousy

One of the leaders of a church I pastored lived next door to the church. She and her children were at the church on a regular basis, but her husband never came. It was generally known that her husband drank too much and hung out with a crowd that was somewhat embarrassing to her, but she held up the family honor and served the Lord to the best of her ability. I once had occasion to visit her in her home. Her children even came in to see me. It was something of a remarkable spectacle to have the pastor visiting in their home. They all had brief conversations with me and went on about their business.

As I sat in the living room and talked to the parishioner, I heard the voice of a man in the next room. The parishioner made no effort to invite the man into the living room or to introduce him to me. I assumed that it was her husband, but I also assumed that her reason for not introducing him was probably because he had been drinking and she would have been embarrassed to have him come in. I finished my visit and left.

By the following Sunday the husband had sent a message to me that I was never to come to his home again for any reason. Since his wife was willing to bring his message to me, I sent one back to him through her. My message was that I would like to talk to him, and I was quite willing to do it at the church if he wanted to come over; but if not, I would have to come back to his house because I had to see him. He invited me back to the house again. Fortunately, this man was straightforward with me and told me immediately when I sat down that he was very angry with me. It didn't seem that he felt that I was doing anything inappropriate with his wife; his issue was that I had come to his home, where he was the head of the household, and I did not even bother to greet him or say anything to him, as if it were not his house at all.

My first inclination was to be like Adam and say, "It was the woman's fault because she did not introduce you to me." Fortunately, I did not fall into that trap. Since my style of ministry is to always develop a relationship, that was the first thing in my mind. I began with how to address him. "By what name should I call you?" was the way I began my response. In a short time we were on a first-name basis, and then I was able to say to him that I respected him as the head of his house. It was not my intent to flatter him, but to call him forth into really being the head of the house, which meant, in my estimation, to become more responsible. We worked through the initial issue of his feel-ing of being ignored and my preferring to relate with his wife instead of him. I thanked him for his honesty and invited him to church again. The next Sunday he showed up at church, dressed appropriately. I daresay he now has a different attitude toward the church and the pastor because of the conversation we had in his home. I am certain that the pastor had a different attitude about him and about visiting in anybody's home.

What I learned from this encounter was that it could have been more serious than it was. Some men can become insanely jealous when the pastor comes to their homes and spends time with their wife. I can hardly believe that I could have been so naïve. Now, whenever I go to any parishioner's home, I ask who is in the house. If it is at all possible, I want to meet everyone who is there. Even if it's only an exchange of names, at least I know I have seen them and expressed some interest in the fact that they live there and that I am a guest in their house.

The second thing I have learned to do is to always develop a general interest in the spouse of any parishioner I visit, even if I am visiting a man, because if I ignore his wife, she may likely experience that as a putdown of her. I make it my business to be interested in them as a couple and a unit as well as individuals. If the spouse knows I am coming and chooses to be away when I am there, I leave a message for the spouse that I was looking for him or her and that I missed him or her when I visited. The most sig-nificant word I have used in this regard is the word *genuine*. If I cannot have *genuine* interest in both persons, I find it very diffi-cult to visit in their home or to even have one of them visit me in my office. This way, especially if the marriage is on the rocks, I express my love and concern equally for both.

Confidentiality

In spite of the fact that the insurance companies would like to have the door open whenever a pastor is talking to an individual, there is still such a thing in pastoral relationships called the "confessional." There are times when a parishioner needs total confidentiality for the purpose of confession. There are legitimate things that people may need to say to their pastors that they don't want anyone else to hear. These things may have to do with their health, financial changes in their lives, or issues related to their family that they are not ready to make public. Sometimes people need the pastor's help when they are trying to surprise their spouse or significant other with, for example, a fiftieth birthday party. I also believe that confession is truly good for the soul. Pastors should, however, avoid being confidants for people who continue to need an excessive amount of privacy. Too much privacy can lead to dangerous situations between pastors and parishioners.

I knew this person who was the first woman pastor of a certain congregation. She was not married, so everybody wanted to be her personal friend. They would tell her things that she was not to tell anybody else. Being trusted felt good to her, so she took on the role of confidant without hesitation. In time the stories became deeper, some verging into pathology. One parishioner knew that her husband was having an affair, but she did not know with whom. She had told the pastor about her concern, but did not want the pastor to say anything yet. The husband told the pastor that he was seeing someone else and planning to get a divorce from his wife. Of course he did not want her to tell anybody. The woman with whom he was having an affair was pregnant; he knew it, but what he didn't know was that the baby was not his. They all had confided in the new female pastor; what a jewel she was!

He finds his pregnant girlfriend in the arms of her baby's father and runs to the pastor for consoling. In the meantime, his wife comes to the parsonage to see the pastor because her husband has gone to be with another woman. She finds her husband being consoled by the pastor, whom she assumes is the other woman. The police had to come and break up the resulting fight; the pastor had to be reassigned; the couple got a divorce; and the whole community, which was very small, was bruised for a few years. Too much secrecy can cause a lot of problems.

A Word About Long-term Counseling

Pastors need to be careful about long-term counseling experiences with parishioners in any setting. Even if they are trained therapists, it is difficult to have a long-term therapeutic relationship and a pastoral relationship with the same person. In most cases I say to people that there is no such thing as absolute privacy. People who do counseling on a regular basis need to have a place where they can share information confidentially among their own professional peers. This is the only way that they can get a peer review and have someone looking over their shoulder to make sure they are not getting caught up in a situation they have not discerned. It is not necessary to share names of persons in these kinds of conferences; however, the dynamics that have taken place between the pastor and his or her parishioner in these private sessions need to be bounced off others who are not involved to maintain objectivity in the relationship.

As long as there is a measure of objectivity, there is a measure of security. Don't fall into the trap of thinking you can handle it alone. You may handle it alone most of the time, but one of these times it will be that very issue that hooks you where you can least afford to be hooked. If you become aware of yourself or the parishioner crossing a boundary, be sure that you do not let this linger for a long time. It conveys a message when that happens and nothing is done or said about it. It is important at the next session for you to talk about crossing the line yourself or to mention the fact that you were uncomfortable that the parishioner had crossed the line. Remember, it is the pastor's responsibility to maintain boundaries. In today's legal climate, while it is human to err and divine to forgive, denominations cannot offer forgiveness to the professional.

RESOURCES

Since every parishioner's home is different, what resources can the pastor turn to in preparation for home visits? The best resources I can think of are senior colleagues' experiences. Talk to others about home visits that they made, the pitfalls that they experienced, and the ways they were able to avoid pitfalls. This is the place where seasoned and retired pastors have a lot to teach younger people in ministry. It is smart to have some of them among your network of colleagues and friends. My own suggestions to pastors about making home visits are to consider home visits like working outside on a very hot summer day. The longer you stay in the sun, the greater the risk of something happening that you would not like to happen. To avoid this risk, plan your work well and work your plan well. Do not go to a parishioner's home not knowing what to say or to do. Be purposeful in the visit to a parishioner's home; and when that purpose is fulfilled, it is time to say good-bye. Be a respectful guest in a parishioner's home. Even though they say, "Make yourself at home," be sure to take that invitation with a grain of salt. If there is anything you need or want, ask permission and assistance. Do not become too comfortable in a parishioner's home. As long as you are experiencing some degree of discomfort, you will be much more careful and cautious in what you do or say. Last, the pastor's responsibility is to bring peace to the home, not destruction or stress or dishonor.

Be sure you are of a peaceful mind when you go to a parishioner's home. It is not a good time to visit a parishioner's home when you have just had a fight with your spouse. It is not a good time to visit a parishioner's home when you have just left an intense committee meeting at the church. It is not a good time to visit a parishioner's home when you are too tired to think straight. And it is especially not a good time to visit a parishioner's home when you are having a crisis of faith, or if you are not sure if you want to stay in the ministry.

Many good pastors have gone before you and done a great job. One of the highest compliments that can be paid to a pastor is "The pastor visited in my home—several times."

THREE

IN THE HOSPITAL

Relationships are all about being *connected*, but pastors must be able and willing to connect in various ways with various people in varying circumstances. This chapter looks at relationships with patients and their families within the context of the hospital. The hospital can be a difficult context for pastoral care, because being hospitalized, whether as a patient or a patient's family, means being disconnected. The hospitalized person is transported into another world, another culture, and thereby disconnected from his or her former status, responsibilities, authority, friends, and much more. Potentially, all of the patient's relationships bear the added burden of emotional, financial, spiritual, sand physical pain. Yet being disconnected also brings the possibility of connecting and reconnecting in new and hopeful ways.

But connections are not automatic, nor do they magically appear. It is the pastor's work to be the channel of God's grace within the confines of the hospital by being aware of the prevailing dynamics to the end that relationships are used to produce fruit of the Spirit—love, joy, generosity, peace, patience, faithfulness, gentleness, kindness, goodness, and self-control (Gal. 5:22-23). The pastor is also called to offer compassion and empathy not only to the patient, but also to the patient's family, and, where appropriate, the hospital staff.

This chapter will look at practical ways pastors can become oriented to hospital culture and establish rapport with the patient, the patient's family, and the hospital staff. It will also briefly discuss the dimensions of pastoral authority within the hospital context and how the pastor can bring comfort to patients through familiar religious rituals such as prayer, baptism, communion, and anointing.

HOSPITAL ORIENTATION

Before a pastor is ready to make a hospital visit, he or she needs to become familiar with the hospital. Hospitals can be strange and scary places to visit if one is not prepared. More is required than reading a book, asking another pastor, or playing it by ear. A hospital is a world in itself. People live minilives in hospitals. The hospital is the place where life begins and ends. In between these natural boundaries is a litany of ups and downs, joys and sorrows, fears, anxieties, frustrations, disappointments, and anger, in addition to often grueling physical pain. Families, friends, and pastors of hospitalized patients may experience these feelings too. Patients themselves experience many of these feelings, but the most frightening is the feeling of being totally alone and totally disconnected from all that is familiar.

In order that the pastor does not further burden the patient and the patient's family and to do an effective job of pastoral care in the hospital, the pastor needs to have a firm grasp of the faces, spaces, places, and graces of the hospital system.

Faces

Faces represent the people who serve in the hospital. These days when budgets are tight, there is no room for anyone on the hospital payroll who does not have an important function. The staff is one large health care team, whether doing surgery or mopping the floor. If pastors see themselves as members of that team and acts accordingly, they will be better able to effectively minister to the patient. To join the team, however, you as the pastor must develop relationships with everyone with whom you have contact. As a cleric, you will know you are accepted as part of the team when staff persons begin to share their own problems and ask for your help and advice.

Most hospital staff members appreciate pastors coming to visit their parishioners, but the staff holds the clergy to a higher standard than other visitors. Clergy are expected to be courteous, polite, cheerful, and obey the rules. In other words, all that is good and holy in the eyes of the hospital. Nevertheless, there are privileges for those who are members of the team, of which the most important is having access to the patient and necessary information about the patient. In most cases, if you ask for information, it will be forthcoming. However, if you do not relate well with the staff, you may find it difficult and frustrating to offer pastoral care, because you will have less access. Remember the faces of the staff and their names as well as you can; be very sure that they will remember yours.

Spaces

If your place of ministry is in a small town, there will be occasions when you have to go to a larger hospital in a nearby (or perhaps not so nearby) city. This is due in part because of economic factors: the trend these days is for larger hospitals to merge with or to acquire smaller hospitals, so there are fewer and fewer small-town hospitals. Many of these smaller hospitals function as outpatient clinics for larger hospitals. More serious problems are sent on to larger hospitals. However, even in larger hospitals the average stay per patient is about four days; it is even shorter in smaller hospitals. Therefore, if the pastor has a chance to visit a patient in the hospital, it most likely will be in a large hospital. Furthermore, the larger the hospital, the more formal the rules and regulations tend to be, unlike the more relaxed atmosphere of the smaller hospital.

Learning the layout of the hospital complex can save precious time and relieve much frustration. Just the size of the hospital can be threatening and overwhelming to many people. Parking space is generally reserved for clergy; however, the clergyperson must usually obtain an identification card to use it. Call ahead. In the hospital there are often spaces to hang up coats and hats, use the phone, meet with family members, find information about parishioners (most often now by computer), and enjoy a cup of coffee. If anything needed is not provided, a good team member has only to ask and most staff persons will try their best to help.

Places

Every patient in the hospital has his own place to be. The family of the patient also has a place to be, and it is important that the family stay in that place or notifies someone when they are leaving. This kind of communication will ensure that the doctor (and you) can find the family if need be. Just as the patient and family have places to be, the pastor does as well. The pastor is not limited to the waiting room as is the family; she or he is allowed in places where family usually cannot go because the pastor's role as team member is respected. Generally the staff members are eager to accommodate pastors, because research indicates that pastoral visits are helpful in hastening recovery from surgery, and because hospitals need to get patients out as quickly as they can for economic and insurance reasons. Beyond that, many people, including the doctor, nurse, nursing aide, social worker, and so forth, see their work in the hospital as a ministry. They identify strongly with pastors, so they like helping pastors do their job.

Outpatient Clinics

One of the disturbing places in all *hospitaldom* is the outpatient clinic. The clinic may or may not be part of the hospital complex. Wherever it is, however, is intended to be less confining, more comfortable, and to deal with less complicated tests and procedures than the hospital. But in these places serious business transpires. Some patients who go in for simple tests are taken straight to the hospital without returning home—and some of them never return home. Letting one's guard down in these facilities is like taking for granted the "friendly" dog that bites you when your back is turned.

Pastors should avoid being lulled into the comfort of believing that the outpatient clinic means a patient's condition is "not really that bad." Most of the time the outpatient's situation is not crucial, but no one can predict when an outpatient's diagnosis will create that one time when pastoral care is needed more than any other time. In fact, fear and anxiety is just as prominent in the outpatient clinic as it is in the hospital; it just isn't talked about as much.

Graces

All pastors have certain gifts and graces: gift of gab, never-meet-a-stranger, good memory for faces or names, humor, warm smiles, and/or compassionate heart. These tools will open many doors for the pastor if they are used well. Many staff and employees in the hospital can benefit when an effective pastor visits. Prayers are often welcome by most staff, regardless of faith tradition. On the other hand, stories abound about pastors who are too single-minded, rigid, businesslike, or obnoxious. The staff and patients hate to see a pastor with such a temperament approaching.

The best way to enhance the gifts one has and become oriented to the hospital culture is by doing a unit of clinical pastoral education (CPE) sometime during training or as a part of continuing education. (I will say more about CPE and continuous education later in this chapter.) There is a great difference in the hospital ministry of those who have experienced CPE and those who have not. If CPE is not an option, the pastor's next best alternative is to take part in the orientation for clergy program (Chaplaincy Open House). Most hospitals have this type of program periodically; if yours does not, you can request it. If there is no formal introductory program, you may request to follow the hospital chaplain around one evening or weekend, or you might team up with another pastor who is more familiar with the hospital. The better oriented you are to the hospital, the better you can use your gifts and graces to do pastoral care.

ESTABLISHING A PASTORAL RELATIONSHIP WITH PATIENTS

Once you have a clear understanding of hospital dynamics, including your membership on the hospital team, you are ready to offer pastoral care to the patient and the patient's family. Connecting at the hospital is different from connecting in another context, such as a potluck dinner, a funeral, or a wedding. It means that no matter how well you may know a person, how good the relationship between you and that individual may be, or how well connected you are, when that person is in the hospital your relationship will change. Effective connection requires a deeper understanding and acceptance of where that person is emotionally, spiritually, relationally, and sometimes physically. Hospitalization often significantly reconfigures your relationship from that point on. One hopes that it will be reconfigured in a positive way, embracing more of God's grace.

While the pastor is not God, the pastor often symbolizes God and bears the brunt of the patient's feelings toward God. But, in any case, the pastor offers the healing and love of God in a concrete relationship. God chooses to work through the compassion and empathy of caring persons to bring health, hope, and peace. Realizing the dire importance of relationships, let us look at developing or deepening a relationship in the hospital setting within the following categories: *commencement, continuation,* and *contingency.*

Commencement

Commencement is beginning a new relationship with someone not known before. In ministry pastors are always meeting someone for the first time. The more you do a good job of caring for people, the more people you will meet for the first time. Parishioners will want you to see their family members, friends will call you to see their friends, strangers will find your name and number and plead for help, and, of course, parents will ask you to see their children. Even if the patient has other pastors visiting, they will still call on you if your style shows that your care comes from your heart. Hence, there will be many opportunities for you to meet and develop new relationships in the hospital.

The Importance of Introductions

People lose everything when they are in the hospital: their space, privacy, clothes, food, schedules, power and authority, sense of control, and even their identity. Often patients are registered by their legal names that are totally different from the names they go by on a daily basis. With so many losses, many patients equate being in the hospital with being in jail. Often patients feel hopeless, ashamed, and guilty for being as depen-dent as they feel in the hospital. The pastor brings a new perspective to the hospital situation. She or he is a sym-bol of authority that is motivated by love, a symbol of hope to allay despair, and a symbol of forgiveness and grace that alle-viates guilt and shame. The pastor can be a manifestation of the familiar and comforting past, which lightens the dark, dreary, and frightening reality of the present. However, be aware that not all persons equate God with love, compassion, and mercy. A frequent question patients ask is, "Why is God punishing me?" The disconnectedness the patient feels may be an opportunity to reconnect with God and others in healthier ways.

Name

Many patients feel like cargo on a ship with only a label and a number, caught in a great storm with no one to hear their pleas for mercy or their cries for just a little humanness. Calm begins to come to the heart and soul of the patient when he or she relates to and uses the name the person uses every day. The person realizes that she or he is more than the number on a bed in a room, that he or she is not just a case or disease. Finally, somebody with some power sees him or her as a person of inherent worth and dignity. The formal "Mr." or "Mrs." gives way to the familiar "Jimmy" or "Geri" in the pastor's greeting. The patient feels, "God really does know me by name. I *am* more than my ailment."

When the pastor gives his own name to the patient, it gives the *patient* a sense of power. It is commonly believed that having someone's name gives one some degree of power over that person. (The Hebrews never spoke God's name because they believed that if a person said it, that person would have power over God or would incur God's wrath for being too forward and disrespectful to God.) On the other hand, hearing one's name is important. Just hearing their names called can make individuals feel better about themselves. Calling the person by a familiar name is a great way to begin a relationship!

Rapport

To establish rapport is to create a space of comfort, warmth, and mutual trust. It begins with respect for and acceptance of the person one encounters. When I worked as a chaplain in a large hospital, I was often called to the emergency room to minister to patients who had been raped. Most of the time the nursing staff would have established rapport with the patient and only called me because the protocol required that a report be written and referrals given. My job was to make sure the patient got everything to which she was entitled. I could always tell by the language on the phone the level of respect the staff had for the victim. They would say, "Chaplain, this poor lady was brutally attacked; could you come please?" There was no question in my mind that they believed her and had empathy for her. As I expected, the woman was usually a well-dressed, educated, articulate person with good manners. She assumed the expected role of a victim and appreciated the nursing staff's care for her.

On the other hand, they might say, "Chaplain, there's a woman down here who claims she has been raped." This woman might have alcohol on her breath, not be dressed well, been out late at night, or for whatever reason may have let the person who attacked her into her house. The staff person showed little, if any, respect for this woman, not even enough to believe her report. In these cases the staff usually establishes no rapport.

When the pastor arrives, the pastor has to establish rapport, especially when the staff has not. Rapport begins with respect for the person with whom you are relating. This means you have to be nonjudgmental, or, at the very least, you must withhold judgment. The pastor must accept each person as she is and where she is. Some pastors have trouble relating to particular patients such as those with HIV or AIDS. They cannot get past the question "How did she get AIDS?" No one asks how someone had a stroke or how she broke a hip? How foolish it would sound if someone asked, "How did you happen to get that cancer?" Yet there are times when pastors cannot establish rapport because the patient feels the pastor's judgment and lack of respect.

Respect of all persons is the entry fee and dues pastors pay to mediate God's grace. To be effective at all, we have to believe that all people are children of God and are due respect. The origin of respect is in our thinking. It is based on a decision that God loves all persons, and, for Christians, that Jesus died for all persons while we were yet sinners (Rom. 5:8). Knowing a person is not a prerequisite for our respect; we can have the same respect for people we have never met or will never meet. However, if that respect is not universal, there will be times when some people will not come under the umbrella of the values that define whom we can respect, and in those cases it will be difficult, if not impossible, to establish rapport.

Acceptance is of the same substance as respect, but has a different flavor; it is closely related to respect, yet a little different. Unlike respect, which comes from the head, acceptance comes from the heart. It is not a universal rule that is applied automatically; it is a warmth and kindness that reserves itself for relationships. This is what Carl Rogers called *unconditional positive regard*, a heart that reaches out and embraces the other without reservation or expectation. While we humans cannot do anything unconditionally, we can do our best and trust God to take care of the rest. Respect is the law; acceptance is love. One can respect and not accept, or accept and not respect, but both are necessary and have to be good enough to establish rapport.

I have learned that people, especially those who have felt a great deal of rejection, can intuit if they are respected and accepted. Even if they do not say anything, they can feel it, especially when rapport is not happening. I once suggested that a man talk to a certain person who I felt might be helpful to him, only to receive the following response, "Ah man, he keeps on talking that smack; he don't know where I'm coming from." My interpretation of what he was saying about the man was "He doesn't respect me." In another situation the person may say, "Nah man, she don't like me anyway." Interpretation: she doesn't accept me. Even if you, the pastor, are misunderstood, if the individual for whom you are trying to care has such a feeling, rapport may be impossible.

Not only do pastors need to *have* respect and acceptance for those whom they pastor, they need to effectively communicate that respect and acceptance. When persons feel accepted by the pastor, they open up their souls to give and receive all that may be shared in the context of that space and time. They become more open to God's healing power. This is rapport at its best: opening possibilities that did not exist before.

Continuation

Continuation occurs when a relationship has already been established and a particular visit is one more episode in an ongoing process of interaction. Here, one needs to attend to the established relationship by deepening and broadening it. It is important to recognize that when a person is in the hospital, he or she is not the person he or she was before. In all new situations, especially threatening ones, people feel anxiety; and anxiety has a way of altering a person's relationships. Generally, anxiety restricts the depth and scope of relationships and causes the person distress. Prolonged anxiety can even cause physical illness, but it would be strange not to experience some anxiety or nervousness when facing a serious challenge, such as hospitalization. While I believe a certain degree of anxiety is always involved in new ventures, it does not have to be debilitating. But you as the pastor must attend to whatever anxiety is present in order to further your relationship with the patient.

Anxiety and fear are not the same things. When people are afraid, they usually know or have a good idea what is frightening them. Their feelings are focused on something. If that something were removed, their fear would be resolved. Anxiety is free-floating. It is a feeling of apprehension, but without focus. It is an uneasiness and nervousness that will not go away, no matter how many things are removed. Since it is not attached to anything in particular, anxiety is difficult to deal with. It can keep people from being able to sleep, and/or cause them to say and/or do things totally out of character. So much energy can be used up when one is anxious that the person can be wiped out, leaving little energy to even fight disease.

When you show up at the hospital to visit someone you already know, you may essentially be meeting a different person. Although *you* may be prepared to meet the person in a certain emotional/spiritual space, the patient may not. The best place to start is in the same place you would start with a new relationship—with the name. This can be a good time to learn more about the patient's name: "Where did your name come from?" "What does your name mean?" "Who gave you your name?" "How do you like your name?" "Do you have a special nickname?" "What were you called when you were growing up?" These and other similar questions show genuine interest in the patient as a person and go a long way to ease anxiety and deepen the relationship.

It is also necessary to establish or reestablish rapport. Such questions as "How long have you lived in this city?" may be very helpful. "How old are your children now?" "Do you have grandchildren yet?" "How are things on the job?" The rule of thumb is to talk about something that does not require a lot of thought, is not too close for comfort considering the circumstances, and something you have in common with the patient. The main thing you are doing is lessening the person's anxiety and building trust. At this point, keep the conversation on the surface until the person is ready to move deeper. What you are doing is preparing the ground for later. Be aware, however, that some conversations will never go beyond this point, and others may leap straight into deep issues.

It is usually a good thing, with any patient that you have known before, to recall the last time you were in conversation. What did you talk about? What were the issues? What did the patient agree to do? Did she follow through? What was the outcome? Of course the pastor should never give the patient the third degree; that destroys trust. All of these and other questions serve to connect the patient to the familiar past. If the patient seems uncomfortable, that line of approach ought to be stopped and replaced by something more agreeable. When the patient is responding freely and especially taking some initiative in the conversation, you can feel your groundwork is paying off and that the patient is ready to go a little deeper. This means rapport is established, and the pastor can move on with the visit.

Contingency

Contingency refers to a person about whom you may know something, although you do not *really* know the person. Often you will be referred to these people. It may be a relative or family member of your parishioner, a friend of a friend, someone the nurse asked you to say hello to while you are in the hospital, someone you used to know but now can barely recall, or someone who called on the phone and said, "Please visit me." These are the kinds of situations you approach with caution and great sensitivity; oftentimes these individuals will expect you to know more about them than you do, and they may expect more of you than you have to give!

Another very important issue is whether individuals to whom you have been referred want you to visit them. Since someone else may have requested your visit, the patient on whom you are calling may not even know that you are coming. They may be irritated at being singled out, or they may feel embarrassed or even ashamed. It is often difficult to do the right thing in these situations, let alone be effective. The pastor is well advised to approach these kinds of situations with much caution. You might find all kinds of land mines.

Since you are beginning with a lot of uncertainty, it is possible your own anxieties and insecurities will be stirred. I tend to forget names if I don't see a person regularly, but I find many people are forgiving and if not forgiving, preoccupied, at least in the hospital, with their own suffering. Just say, "Let's you and I start all over (or start out fresh) and get to know each other." Once that is said, treat this situation as if you were meeting them for the first time. Regardless of what someone else may have told you about this patient, be open to hearing it directly from the patient. Your relationship may be different than someone else's. Give yourself and the patient a chance to build whatever relationship you can.

ESTABLISHING A PASTORAL RELATIONSHIP WITH FAMILIES

I have intentionally focused first and foremost on the pastor's introduction and establishing rapport with the patient, because the patient is the owner of his or her life and body. Up to and including death, the patient's own wishes for his or her body carry the greatest weight in medical decisions and even court cases. However, when people become patients, they often lean heavily on their families for support and care, especially in decision making. Even when people are quite alert and competent, many family members think they are being helpful by assuming or sharing the patient's decision making; others will try to usurp the patient's right to make his or her own decisions. The point is that it is most likely that when you visit a patient in the hospital, you will encounter family members. Pastoral care with families in the hospital context means knowing a little about family leadership dynamics, realizing that building rapport is an ongoing process, and facilitating the flow of information to the family.

Families need care because they are caught up in a situation that is out of their control. They have fear, anxiety, anger, and other feelings that can interfere and complicate an already stressful situation for the patient if they are not dealt with. Some families may even try to prevent the patient from receiving pastoral care. Once, when I arrived to see my parishioner, family members met me and stated the patient did not want to see me. While I knew this was untrue, I also did not want to make a scene. Later I found a note on the door saying no one was to visit, including the pastor, without first getting permission from the family. While in this case I was not surprised by the family's behavior, suffice it to say that if the pastor does not develop a positive relationship with the family, the pastor may not have a chance to provide the pastoral care that the patient needs and wants.

You can use the same process to establish relationship with the family as you use to develop a relationship with the patient. The difference is, however, that a family is much more complex than an individual. A family may have multiple languages, educational backgrounds, vocational interests, religious values, and differing expectations of you and God. How, then, does one approach such a beast? With the patient you begin with an introduction; with the family you must first identify to whom to address your introduction. You must first locate the family leader.

Family Leadership

Every family has a leader. The pastor must respect that leader, because he or she represents that family's system of operation. It is best to work with the leader of the family in all matters, and it may well be the only way to do any work at all.

As you approach a family to establish a relationship, you will do the same thing that you do when you establish a relationship with one person. You introduce yourself to every family member present and learn each person's relationship to the patient. Often one person will introduce everybody and tell how he or she is related. Sometimes you will have to make individual introductions one by one, but it must be done; and you must be careful not to exclude anyone, not even the children. The ritual of introduction may be a very sensitive time for some of the family members; and the one excluded, even unintentionally, may be the leader or intimately related to the leader of the family. More important, everyone needs to feel that he or she has a respected place. What you are doing, among other things, is affirming connections and connectedness in a hospital context where disconnectedness is the norm.

It is important to identify the leader of the family as soon as possible. To help in this regard, the pastor may ask some general questions, such as "Do all of you live near here?" "How long have you been here at the hospital?" "Can I get anything for anybody?" "Are they telling you what is going on?" This gives the pastor a chance to see without being intrusive the nonverbal responses as well as hear the answers. Such responses help the pastor realize who the leader of the family is. For example, usually everyone will look at the leader, assuming he or she will answer the questions. If anyone other than the leader answers, that responder will look at the leader as if to see if he has "permission" to answer. Sometimes a family has a spokesperson who is not the leader. That person may do the talking, but only with the permission of the leader, who may be sitting quietly, as if not leading the family.

If the leader is not in the room, there may be uneasiness about answering any question. They will say, "We have to wait until (John) comes" or "We need to talk about it," which means the same thing. They will not decide on their own without consultation with the leader of the family. Sometimes there is a resistance on the part of the leader to take authority. On the other hand, there are those who are only too eager to take authority. Ultimately, family members demonstrate by their behavior who their leader is, even if it is only in this current situation. They will follow only the true leader. I have sat with many families at the death of a patient. I always watch for the dynamics of leadership. If the person who died was the leader, some family members will be a little confused. Out of those chaotic times, however, you may witness the birth of a new family leader. For instance, different family members may suggest going home, but no one moves. Finally, the leader will speak or stand up, and everybody gets up and goes home.

Rapport Is an Ongoing Process

Rapport with the family is an ongoing process; thus, they need to have their care coordinated with the patient's. If there is no coordination of pastoral care, there is the risk that the family will, intentionally or unintentionally, sabotage or disconnect from the work that the pastor is doing with the patient. While a medical problem brought the patient to the hospital, the dynamics of deep emotions and scary thoughts take over soon after the patient enters the hospital. The medical team is in charge, but the pastor is also part of that hospital care team; and the goal of the team is to get everybody through the crisis of illness with the least amount of anguish, while maintaining rapport.

Rapport Means Facilitating the Flow of Information

Next to the medical treatment of the patient, the next most powerful dynamic in the hospital is the flow of information. Information, or the lack of information, is responsible for many of the feelings that patients and families have in the hospital. Problems arise when the flow of information is cut off or when the information is inconsistent. This is why it is so important that the pastor relate to both the family and the patient. The pastor can help keep the flow of information timely and consistent. This minimizes the possibility of friction arising between the patient, various factions of the family, and the staff. The relationship that you develop with both the patient and the family gives you a level of trust and consequently a powerful role. Facilitating communication is the natural role of a pastor. You may not need rapport to share good news, but it is essential when the news is bad.

ESTABLISHING A PASTORAL RELATIONSHIP WITH STAFF

To have staff cooperation and access to information in the hospital, the pastor needs to have rapport with the hospital staff. The staff is a team that has interdependent members; each person has some power to make things happen. I worked as a chaplain in a major hospital for more than twenty years, and I found that I could get anything I needed and/or wanted through having good relationships with the staff. When I visited other hospitals, I noticed I could get anything I needed, even though I was a stranger. No one ever asked me for identification when I said I was a minister. The staff imputed a degree of team status to me, simply because I conformed to their expectations of what a minister looked and acted like. Most likely I benefited from other ministers' rapport building. But building rapport takes time and energy.

The pastor can develop a relationship with hospital staff by using the same process that is so effective in relating to patients and family members. Staff people can feel helpless. Often they cannot get away from watching patients, some of whom may be dying and nothing can be done about it. They see family members in pain and wish they could give them comfort. They know the circumstances that brought particular cases to the hospital; sometimes it is senseless tragedy. They know how doctors and other staff people have treated particular patients and families. Often they wish the hospital had been more sensitive. Sometimes they know mistakes have been made, to the patient's detriment. The staff hopes you will be sensitive. Perhaps you will say a kind word, offer a special prayer, or just wish everyone a good day. You may think that you are there only to see your parishioner, but the staff may see you as an answer to their prayers. So often, as a caring pastor, all that is necessary is to introduce yourself and ask, "How are you today?"

Often staff members are very busy, but being too busy to talk is often the way they deal with their feelings: they work them off. If they are too busy to talk because of demanding tasks, they definitely have some feelings about that. While it is not a good thing to push oneself on busy staff persons, you can break through this wall with patience. You need to simply introduce yourself and acknowledge how busy the person is. You can then announce, "I would like a few words with you about (name the patient) when you have a moment," and stand or sit in plain view patiently until the staff person comes to you.

If you do not have the time to wait on this occasion, you need to introduce yourself and say, "Is there a time when we can talk about (name the patient)?" Being respectful and polite speaks volumes to staff members. Show concern for them and offer to keep them in your prayers. The better you relate to the staff, the better the staff will relate to your parishioner. Developing good rapport with the staff also builds the pastor a reputation as a minister who cares about his or her congregants. The staff will respect you and may respond with acceptance and understanding when you need it.

PASTORAL AUTHORITY

While pastors have definite authority in the world of the parish, in the hospital, the pastor has very little, if any, formal authority. The hospital is a world of science and medicine; the doctor is its god. Pastors may have respect in the hospital, but no authority. Some authority is invested in the nurses, but they get their authority from the doctor. This is not only a tradition in medicine; it is a legal issue as well. The pastor will not lose his or her license because of what happens to a patient in the hospital, but doctors and nurses can. They are legally responsible for the patient and all of the care that the patient receives or does not receive in the hospital. Nevertheless, the pastor may be granted informal authority that involves the pastor's perspective and the power to facilitate the patient's follow-up care.

Authority of Perspective

Aside from legal authority, the medical field has the authority of knowledge. All of society looks to them for the answers to our medical questions. When someone is sick, it is our society's belief that the doctor is the one who can make that person well again. In past years, the doctor had absolute authority. That has changed over the last fifteen to twenty years because of issues surrounding medical ethics. When Harvard Medical School offered another definition of death (brain death) different than the one that had been used in the past (no heart beat), we entered a new era of medical science. Doctors did not feel comfortable pronouncing patients dead when their hearts were still beating (most often with the help of a respirator). Some family members would sue if the doctor did not stop every treatment procedure soon enough, and others would sue if the doctor stopped too soon. Doctors began inviting family members to take part in the decision about when to *"pull the plug,"* as they called it.

Pastors are often welcome to join in this decision-making process on behalf of the family. It is often a difficult decision for all concerned. Although the pastor has no defined authority in the hospital, the pastor can have great influence on what happens. The influence of the pastor is based on his or her ability to develop and maintain rapport. Pastors can also be very helpful keeping the discussion focused on the people involved. This authority that is derived from perspective is much needed and often well received.

Authority to Facilitate Follow-up Medical Care

Another area in which the pastor may have informal authority in the hospital is related to follow-up care. As I stated earlier, the average hospital stay is about four to four and a half days. Whatever is done or not done in the hospital will rise or fall based on the follow-up care of the patient. The follow-up care may or may not be medical in nature. The important issue is who will be available to assist the patient or to ensure that whatever the patient needs is provided. Once the patient leaves the hospital, for all practical purposes the doctor has no more authority. The doctor can write prescriptions but cannot be sure that they will be filled. The consultation, instructions, and recommendations that the hospital staff gives may or may not be followed.

Some years ago a young man was in the heart transplant program at the hospital where I was a chaplain. He missed an appointment, which was a serious no-no. A nurse scheduled another appointment, which he also missed. When they finally got him to the hospital, she called me to help impress on him the seriousness of these appointments. When I spoke to him, we learned that he had realized how critical his appointments were and tried not to miss them. However, his aunt, who had agreed to bring him to his appointments, changed her mind at the last minute. The nurse said to him, "Why did you not just pick up the phone and call? We could have sent a taxi to pick you up and bring you to your appointment." The young man replied, "We don't have a phone." The nurse asked why he had not told her before what the problem was. He said he didn't know, but he had meant to tell her. My interpretation was—knowing this nurse as I did—the conversation with her was always about the medical issues, not the personal ones.

She had labeled this patient noncompliant and was about to give up on him because he would not cooperate. I was able to get a church involved with this young man. In other words, I connected him with people who could help him. His disconnectedness with his family provided a church with the opportunity to connect him to a better life. They took him on as a mission project and saw to it that he had no more transportation problems. The transplant program also helped him find more suitable housing with a phone and helped him to begin taking college classes. Pastors can make a difference if they are willing to work as team members with other professionals for the good of the patient.

Pastors can also help connect patients to new lives as participating members of society.

RITUALS AND ETIQUETTE

The pastor brings to the hospital the familiar symbols, icons, and rituals that are of great comfort to patients when they are facing challenging times in their lives. Just the mention of "Pastor," "Minister," Reverend," "Priest," "Father," "Rabbi," or some other familiar title can bring peace to an anxious soul in a hospital bed. The title will change according to the culture, tradition, or congregation; however, the dynamic is the same. Some Christian traditions use the symbol of the cross extensively; others use oil for anointing. Lighting of candles is very prominent in some faiths. Various rituals or prayer books are used by most traditions. It is not unusual to find a blessed blanket, scarf, or other items that give comfort to patients. In this section I will discuss offering the rituals of prayer, baptism, communion, and anointing.

Prayer

The most frequently used religious ritual in the hospital is prayer. All faiths and traditions have some form of prayer that they use for people who are sick. Some have special prayers for patients who are hospitalized. Prayers may be written or taken from books that provide prayers for all occasions, or prayers may be spontaneous. Each pastor has his own style of prayer in the hospital. Patients expect their pastors to pray for them appropriately. Some patients request prayers from as many people as they can and for as many different forms of prayer as they can get. I would often visit with patients who would say, "My pastor has already been here and prayed, but you can pray too." Some request prayers from traditions other than their own.

I once visited a person from the Middle East who was a Muslim. He could not speak English, but his daughter had come to the United States with him to translate. When I first met him, she was not around. He gestured to me to pray for him. The next day when I returned, I met his daughter. She thanked me for praying for her father and wanted me to know that, although he was receiving prayers from the Muslim community, he wanted me to continue to come and pray for him every day. It is not uncommon for patients to desire daily prayer from as many different ministers and other people as they can get.

Prayers ought to be appropriate. *Canned* prayers are usually too general to speak to the issue at hand. Prayer should not be substituted for the pastoral care that is needed and desired. Do not use prayer to avoid talking to the patient. Some pastors rarely pray unless it is specifically requested. My own thoughts are that it is more helpful to the patient if he or she first has a chance to talk about the problem that needs prayer. Once the patient has shared those feelings, the pastor may then pray more specifically for the patient and the issues the patient is facing. Each patient needs his or her own prayers. It is also comforting to most patients to know that the pastor will continue to pray for them.

Baptism

Another common ritual is baptism. Baptism is extremely prevalent in the newborn units of the hospital, but it also happens in other places as well. When a baby who may have some medical problems is born, often parents and other family members want the baby baptized to ensure that if the baby dies, he or she will go to heaven. Actually, Protestants generally believe that baptism is for the purpose of initiating the baby—or anyone else—into the faith community of the church. However, try telling that to the parents who are about to lose their baby. Even parents whose tradition does not baptize babies often request baptism when death is anticipated.

It is not a good thing to simply say, "We do not baptize babies," and let it go at that, just as it is not good to refuse to help a grieving family that requests baptism of someone who is already dead. Nor is it the time to educate people about which tradition allows or does not allow what. What is important is that the pastor get an understanding of what the family wants and needs and offer prayers that are meaningful and bring comfort to the family. Most families are satisfied knowing that this is not a traditional baptism, but a petition to God to look favorably on the deceased.

While it is true that some traditions recognize only immersion as the form of baptism, that form of baptism is difficult to do in the hospital. However, it has been done, and I reiterate that nurses are the best assistants that a pastor can find in the hospital. They will help with any form of baptism they can, even to the point of helping to find a way to immerse a patient. However, even if the facility is available for immersion, the patient may be too sick. What you can do is remind the person and the family that if the thief on the cross was acceptable to God with no baptism at all, surely there is some way the patient can be made acceptable to God without being buried in water.

Communion

Far more common in the hospital than baptism is the ritual of Christian communion. Some traditions provide communion every day when a person is in the hospital. Others bring communion only once, no matter how long a person may be hospitalized. Still others do not believe that communion can be taken in any context other than in the communion service at church. It may surprise you that patients and family members are not actually interested in the theology and traditions that determine when, where, or how they may receive communion. They are only interested in how they can get through the next day of hospitalization and what will give them the most peace during their stay. Last, many want to make sure that they have done all that is required of them in the event of death.

Although prayers are usually accepted from anyone, members of some traditions, such as Roman Catholics, and Missouri Synod Lutherans, will usually not receive communion from someone who is not of their tradition. Although these traditions will not receive communion *from* anyone out of their tradition, some pastors in those traditions will serve communion *to* persons who are not of their traditions. Although these practices may be debatable, the hospital is not the place or the time to raise these arguments. These rituals serve to connect the patient and the patient's family to the faith community and to God. However, if *you* are uncomfortable in offering communion to a particular person, pray that the elements will be received with an appropriate attitude.

Anointing

The concept of anointing with oil goes a long way back. To anoint someone was to set that person apart; to empower that individual to do great feats; to protect the person from enemies and other foes; and to acknowledge the individual's saving power and influence for a community, a people, or a nation. It is no wonder the Christian community embraces this rite and uses it during times of illness. Not all traditions use anointing of the sick, even though they may believe in it doctrinally. Some traditions even go to great lengths to procure the appropriate oil for this rite. After you bless the oil, you smear it or make the sign of the cross with it on the patient's forehead with words of blessing. Many believe this rite brings to the patient healing and protection from evil.

Closely associated with anointing with oil is the laying on of hands. Sometimes both are done at the same time, and sometimes laying on of hands is done without anointing oil. In the Christian concept of anointing, there is the belief that the Holy Spirit anoints people; this suggests that anointing can, and does, take place without the benefit of oil. To lay on hands and pray is a request for God's anointing. With or without oil (some pastors always have anointing oil in their possession), anointing is a powerful ritual that is used in the hospital. This ritual is even more common now than it was about fifteen years ago, because of the insurgence of the evangelical movement in this country and around the world.

Anointing is safer and more convenient in the hospital than either baptism or communion. Unlike baptism, which is usually done once in a lifetime, anointing can be done over and over again. It is not as controversial as communion, since it is not considered a sacrament by many people. As it is, there are few limits or requirements placed on this practice. However, anointing is not for everybody. Some people continue to be uncertain of its theological meaning and do not want to take any risks with their souls, which is their right and choice.

Sometimes well-meaning family members will make a request for a patient who cannot speak for himself or herself. All religious rituals should be held to the same standard as any other ethical issue. If the patient would not request or receive a particular religious rite, that patient should not be taken advantage of when she is not in a position to refuse even if it is believed by family or anyone else that a particular rite would save the patient's life or soul. Religion is always voluntary, and the benefits are not ever to be forced on someone or given in a fraudulent way.

DILEMMAS

A couple of years ago, one of my students, who happened to be a Roman Catholic sister, brought a case to the CPE group that really disturbed her. She was the chaplain on call at a major hospital and was called to minister to a family, which happened to be Catholic. The patient was a young girl who was the victim of trauma and her family was with her. The student asked if the family wanted a priest. (Catholics have for years performed last rites for people who were about to die. That is not the case anymore, but some Catholics do not know that.) The parents of the child said no, they did not want a priest. We in the CPE group surmised that in the mind of the parents, to have a final rite of any sort would mean they had given up on the child recovering.

In the room an aunt of the child took the chaplaincy student aside and demanded that a priest be called. When the chaplain told the aunt the inappropriateness of doing that, the woman went to the nursing staff and made the same demand. They told her the chaplain would take care of that. At this point the woman went to a private phone and called a priest, who came and went directly into the room without the parents' knowledge and performed last rites on the child. As he was leaving, the chaplain saw him and questioned his being there. He said, "I have taken care of that little girl." The chaplain was livid with anger and disappointment. When she pointed out to him that the parents of the girl had requested that this not happen, he responded, "I know, but she needed it."

This case in no way represents the excellent ministry that most Roman Catholic priests do, but it does point out that there are ministers in every tradition who believe so strongly in the efficacy of their rituals that they surrender their integrity in the name of good, better, and best. No pastor should ever perform a rite on a minor without the parents' consent.

Another Example

A man was in what turned out to be the last two hours of his life. His family was with him and he had become uncommunicative. One of his daughters talked to the chaplain and explained that her father had never been baptized, and she was concerned about his soul. The chaplain tried to comfort her as much as possible, and the daughter stated she felt better. A few minutes later, she requested that the man be baptized. The chaplain tried to explain that the man would have to agree to this, and he was well past that point now. The daughter's reply was that he had signed an advanced medical directive that gave her the authority to make decisions for him in the event he could not do so himself. In the course of the conversation, the chaplain asked what she thought would be accomplished by baptizing him now. She believed God would receive him more favorably if he were baptized. The alert chaplain took her to the bedside and said a prayer that God would receive this man with favor.

Appropriately no baptism was performed, and also appropriately the family was ministered to in a comforting manner. Religious rituals are very powerful and meaningful tools of ministry, but rituals are made for people, not people for rituals.

ADDITIONAL HOSPITAL RESOURCES

Hospitals are usually eager to help pastors do their work with patients. Nurses will provide space and privacy for prayer; there are usually small quiet rooms available for prayer and consultation. Nurses will usually provide distilled water for baptisms, especially in the newborn units. Cameras are often available for these occasions. Most hospitals have a spiritual care department which will provide communion kits and often anointing oil, if needed. Beyond helping the pastor who is present, the hospital is also willing to help the pastor who cannot get to the hospital. If someone needs anointing, baptism, communion, or prayer, and the pastor cannot come or there is no pastor, the hospital can often provide this service.

The hospital will also through the pastoral or spiritual care department notify the patient's pastor that the patient is in the hospital. Some hospitals do this automatically unless a request is made not to do it; others will do so only upon request. The service is there for the asking. While in the hospital, patients have available most any religious need that they may have. The hospital either has chaplains on staff who are trained to do whatever is needed, or it will contact someone to serve patients' religious needs. There are patients in rare cases who have even been able to get married in the hospital. It may surprise the average person how often this could happen, if it were not discouraged.

One of the best ways to learn about hospital ministry and develop skills in hospital ministry is to take at least one unit of clinical pastoral education. CPE is a standardized process of learning pastoral care under supervision and with a group of peers. There are over three hundred accredited centers across the country where CPE training is available. It consists of seminars relating to pastoral care, interpersonal group relations, and pastoral care visits to patients in hospitals with individual and group supervision of the entire process. Four hundred hours of group experience and hands-on ministry comprise one unit of training. Most major hospitals around the country are at least familiar with the Association for Clinical Pastoral Education, the association that accredits the centers where CPE training takes place and certifies the supervisions who do the training.

CONCLUSION

Building pastoral relationships in the hospital means that the pastor must be aware of the dynamics of the hospital culture through faces, spaces, places, and graces. The pastor gains entry to the health care team primarily by the skill in establishing rapport with the patient, the patient's family, and the staff. This rapport comes under the rubrics of *commencement, continuation,* and *contingency.* While these rubrics are important in offering pastoral care to staff, patients, and patients' families, the pastor must also be aware of the dynamics of family leadership while also recognizing that the family leader is sometimes the gatekeeper to patient pastoral care. As a member of the health care team, the pastor's authority is informal and exerted through influence, rather than formal and exerted through hospital rules. Although ill-defined, this informal authority and established rapport of the pastor enables him or her to connect the patient with others inside and outside of the hospital, including God.

One way the pastor can connect or reconnect the patient to God and the family of faith is through familiar religious rituals such as prayer, baptism, communion, and anointing. But sometimes a few moments of quietness is the most meaningful and connecting thing a pastor can do. The hospital is a little world to itself, a world that, through relationship, the pastor can effectively incarnate the ever-willingness of God to connect with us.

FOUR

IN THE NURSING HOME

Some years ago in Indianapolis, Indiana, I was preaching at a church that also operated a nursing home. This nursing home building was the first building designed and built in Indiana to be a nursing home. There were several other nursing homes in the city, but those buildings had been converted from some other use and made into nursing homes. This indicates how uncommon nursing home facilities were a few years ago. Today nursing homes abound throughout the country. They used to be available for only a small percentage of the elderly population, but today many more elderly people will spend their last days in a nursing home.

There are a lot of reasons nursing homes are more prevalent today: (1) People are living longer and at some point just become too old and feeble to care for themselves; (2) children are much more mobile and family members are not as available to care for the elderly as they once were; (3) sometimes living in a nursing home provides a more stable environment than living with family members; and (4) there is even some support for the idea that elderly people appreciate other people with whom they have more in common. Whatever the reason may be, people in ministry today will likely be making visits to a nursing home to see their parishioner or someone their parishioner has requested they visit.

ESTABLISHING A PASTORAL RELATIONSHIP

One of the things the minister needs to keep in mind when visiting residents in a nursing home is that although the residents may be physically ill, they may be very alert and mentally sound. I have visited many people in nursing homes over the years and have had many pleasant, sometimes challenging, conversations with them. It is a mistake to assume that because a person is in a nursing home, he or she will not be able to carry on a normal conversation. The pastor should approach the situation with the expectation of developing a pastoral relationship with this parishioner just like any other parishioner, only that this parishioner happens to live in a nursing home.

Another thing that residents in a nursing home need, and rarely have, is a person who will listen to what they have to say. It is not uncommon to find people in their upper eighties and nineties in nursing homes. These persons have lived long lives and have a lot of experience to talk about. There is much to be learned from them if one will take the time to listen. If you want to establish rapport with a nursing home resident, it's important that you are patient enough to listen to what the person has to say.

I had a discussion with a group of students recently about visiting patients in a retirement center that included an assisted-living facility. One of the students insisted that the task of the chaplain was to identify the problem that the person may have

and to help the person find a solution. Some pastors have difficulty establishing rapport with people in nursing homes because
they are simply looking for a particular problem they can fix.
Here is an example:

A rabbi hated to visit a ninety-six-year-old resident in a nursing home; it seemed that even though the resident was very alert,
the elderly man would not talk about anything that was personal.
His family was concerned about his health and his future, but he
had very little to say. It was very boring to sit with him and not
know what to talk about. I responded to my friend, the rabbi,
in two ways: How can a pastor not feel privileged to spend time
with a ninety-six-year-old man, especially one that is alert and
able to converse? And second, when a man is ninety-six years
old, the future is not necessarily what he wants to focus on; most
of his life is in his past. What a great opportunity to learn from
someone who has lived through ninety-six years of experience!
Establishing rapport is not difficult when the pastor is parish-
ioner-centered.

Another student said that it was frustrating when he tried to
find out what was going on with the residents, because they kept
insisting, "I like it here; things are wonderful here; I'm very happy
here." In the first place, elderly people do not always see problems
the way that younger people do. Many of them have endured
much more hardships than younger generations may ever experience. As they got older, their desires and needs became fewer in
terms of what it takes to make them feel content. It's difficult to
be problem-focused and try to establish rapport with anybody,
especially people in a nursing home, if all you are looking to do
is fix them.

But probably the most common issue in a nursing home as far
as residents are concerned is loneliness. Family members often
live in different states; even those who live close by do not visit
very often. Friends and neighbors who were so attentive before
the person went to a nursing home often cannot or will not visit
them in the nursing home. It is rare that residents in a nursing
home have all the visitation they want or need. Any indication
on the part of the pastor that he or she will be visiting a nursing

home resident on a regular basis will go a long way in establishing a pastoral relationship. It is also helpful to take something with you to the nursing home if you want to establish an abiding relationship. It's not a gift that costs a lot of money that makes a difference: it could be a bulletin from the church, a greeting card, something that they may be able to eat, flowers, and so forth, anything that lets the person know that you and the church community have been thinking about him. These tokens can also serve as a remembrance of your visit after you have gone and as a reminder that someone cares during those lonely times.

When I was on the board of one nursing home, I became aware that one of the most common and frustrating problems in the nursing home was petty theft committed by other nursing home residents. They took things that were rarely anything of monetary value: They would pick up little items such as flowers, cards, the kinds of things that are listed in the above paragraph that you might bring to the resident when you visit. Some residents who did not usually get a visit or who would not have any of these things in their own room would simply pick them up wherever they saw them. This was very frustrating to the other residents for many reasons, including an invasion of their privacy, because these little things taken were not little in their eyes.

ESTABLISHING A PASTORAL RELATIONSHIP WITH THE RESIDENT'S FAMILY

Nursing homes usually have much more lenient visiting hours than hospitals. In a nursing home, anyone can visit any time he or she would like; consequently, a pastor may visit a resident many times and never see a family member there. It may be necessary for you to contact the family members on the phone or have them visit you in your office. It is important, however, that you have a relationship with the resident's family members, whether or not the resident is a member of the congregation.

In establishing rapport with family members, the pastor needs to realize that the issues that family members struggle with are different from those of the resident. While the resident may be dealing with loneliness, family members often deal with guilt: guilt because they helped make the decision to put the resident in the nursing home; guilt because they have not been able to visit as much as the resident would like and perhaps needs; guilt because this may be a parent, grandparent, aunt, or uncle who has given all that he or she had for the family member to have a good life, and the family member feels that gift is not being returned in the same measure or in the same way.

Other feelings that family members may be struggling with are anxiety and fear. Many negative stories abound about nursing homes, and family members often wonder what will happen to their loved one when they are not around. They may also wonder how they are seen in the eyes of others, for example, the pastor, in relation to their decision to put their loved one in the nursing home in the first place. To establish rapport with family members, it is important that family members know the pastor does not judge the decision about putting their loved one in a nursing home. Often people will begin the conversation with the pastor by saying, "We tried everything we could, but we just could not do any better," and listing reasons why they had no choice but to put the person in a nursing home. This should be an indication to the pastor that there is some anxiety and fear of judgment from the pastor about their decision. The pastor needs to reassure the family members that their decision is not being questioned or judged. Good, empathic responses to their statements go a long way in establishing good rapport. For example, when they list the many ills that their loved one has and how difficult it was to care for them, the pastor might respond, "It certainly put a lot of demands on you, didn't it?"

ESTABLISHING A PASTORAL RELATIONSHIP WITH THE STAFF

As I stated in chapter 3, it is always important to have a pastoral relationship with the staff. I suggest to my clinical pastoral education students when they are assigned to a hospital unit to always develop a relationship with the unit secretary first. The same thing holds true for nursing home ministry. Develop a solid relationship with the unit secretary first. Some people believe that they get the best results if they talk to the doctor, the nurse, or the administrator. My experience is that most of the communication goes through the staff person who sits at the reception desk in the unit. Regardless of who is giving the orders, who is in charge, or what might be happening, the person sitting in that chair is *the* coordinator of everything that is happening in that area. If a resident is taken away, this staff person knows where the resident is going and when the resident will be back. If someone had a visitor this morning, the staff person usually knows about that visitor as well. If someone failed to eat his or her food, the staff person has to put that in the chart. Anything that goes on with any of the residents usually runs through this staff person, because everything has to be noted in the resident's records. If you develop a good relationship with this person as you come in, you will have access to most anything in the area. The flip side of this is that if you do not develop a good relationship with this staff person, you may experience a lot of resistance to the simplest request.

The best way to establish rapport with staff people in the nursing home is to show some interest in them as persons. Some people will walk in and simply ask where a particular resident is or how to find a certain room number, and so forth. It is very important that you introduce yourself to staff members you meet and ask genuinely how they are doing. Working in a nursing home can be a thankless job at times, and it goes a long way when a pastor takes an interest in the person who is working there. Even though staff persons may protest that they are very busy, it doesn't take much time to exchange names and some things of interest between you. What you need to keep in mind is that staff rapport is not an option; it is absolutely necessary to be able to provide pastoral care to residents. Since people who work in nursing homes are usually poorly paid and required to care for persons in many ways that we might find distasteful, they look forward to those rare occasions when someone like a pastor comes along and affirms what they are doing and affirms them as people. This establishes a high level of rapport and a deep level of trust.

Authority

Many pastors are afraid to visit nursing homes because they feel that they have no authority. This is because they misunderstand what it means to have authority. Rarely will a pastor find the opportunity to exercise as much authority as he or she may exercise in a nursing home. There are several reasons why pastors have power in nursing homes: (1) A pastor's authority comes from God. If we believe the Scriptures, we understand that God has a special place in God's heart for elderly and powerless people. The pastor has authority in a nursing home because this is where God wants the pastor to be. God wants to use the pastor to manifest God's promise of never leaving and never forsaking those who have put their faith in God. When you enter a nursing home, you can be sure that you are in a place where God would have you be.

(2) The pastor has authority in the nursing home because there is little competing authority. In other places like the hospital, pastors may run into other pastors while they are making their visits. However, in the nursing home the field is wide open. The staff enjoys having pastors in the nursing homes and the residents enjoy having the pastors. People who work in the nursing home are usually paid at the lower level of the pay scale. Many of them could find positions that would pay more money; however, their sense of mission calls them to work in places where so many people are in such need. Since their mission is to help elderly people feel better in whatever way they can, these employees enjoy seeing the pastor come, because they believe the pastor not only shares the same mission but also helps them fulfill theirs.

Recently I took a group of laypeople to a nursing home. The administrator was overjoyed to have us come and visit. Although he was not clear what we would do while we were there, just the fact that we were there and visible to the residents was a blessing in itself. As it turned out, we were standing in a parlor next to the dining room, so we began to sing songs—hymns that were familiar to the residents. Some of the residents had already begun to come down for supper, but when they heard the music they went back and called other residents to come and hear the music. Before long, we had a crowd of people smiling, singing, and enjoying themselves. After several songs, we took a break and walked around and talked to people individually. They enjoyed the visits as much as they did the music. We prayed, recited scriptures, and sang a few more songs; then we said our good-byes. We were hailed as angels from heaven by both the residents and the staff for having come to the nursing home and spending time with the people there.

(3) What happened in that nursing home was made possible by one person, the pastor. The pastor has authority in the nursing home because he or she has access to other people. The pastor acts as a bridge to the broader faith community who can brighten the lives of the residents and staff. Without the blessing and encouragement of pastors, few people would visit the nursing home. As a pastor you carry a wealth of religious tradition that includes songs, Scriptures, prayers, and innumerable relationships that can minister to the needs of nursing home residents.

While *authority* means to have power, control, prerogative, and so forth, it also means to increase, promote, and make many. Power in itself is of little value unless one uses that power in a productive way. The value of power in a nursing home is that the pastor can empower those who are there. The pastor can empower the staff and the residents. This is what it means to increase and make many: to promote by sharing the power and authority that the pastor has with those who have less. The pastor empowers by acceptance and affirmation. In a nursing home, many people are struggling to survive and find a place of comfort from very challenging situations.

Nursing homes can also be ethically challenging places. The nursing home is often a place "in between"; it is a part of society and yet apart from society. It can be a place where the black and white principles of right and wrong or helpful and hurtful exist merely in shades of gray. There is no textbook that says, "Do ABC and the result will be XYZ." Many decisions are made on the spur of the moment with the hope that they will be beneficial to the resident, the family, and the staff. Sometimes staff people tell stories about how they dealt with a question of what was the right thing to do. The pastor has the authority to bless and authorize anything that promotes genuine love and caring, just as Jesus stated in the Scriptures: Whatever you loose on earth will be loosed in heaven, and whatever you bind on earth will be bound in heaven (Matt. 16:19). He also says: Whom the Son sets free is free indeed (John 8:36). So it is with the pastor in the nursing home: whatever the pastor affirms in the nursing home carries great weight. There can be so much love and acceptance of a pastor in a nursing home that it is difficult to be anything other than authoritative.

RITUALS AND ETIQUETTE

One of the benefits of being part of a faith community for many years is that when people become elderly and their mind begins to play tricks on them (to say the least), memories of traditions from the faith community will come back to them when nothing else can. I have visited people in nursing homes and my students have reported many situations where people were quite limited mentally but still able to understand and appreciate rituals like the Lord's Supper, prayer, singing hymns, and reading Scriptures. These kinds of behaviors have been embedded so deeply in their hearts and minds that not even dementia can destroy their awareness and appreciation. Even when they can no longer hold an intelligible conversation, they still know to bow their heads in a prayerful attitude when prayer is offered.

Handshaking

Few of us think of handshaking as a ritual; however, handshaking is one of the most common and most powerful rituals that we practice in our culture. The clasping of hands in prayer, the reaching out of one's hand to shake hands when meeting a new person, and the last touch before the parting handshake after having spent time with a person are very meaningful rituals. Handshaking is a ritual that is universal in Western culture and exists in some other form in many other cultures. It is so deeply engrained that it requires no thought or decision to participate. It is literally automatic for many people in appropriate situations. This simple ritual is much more powerful in a nursing home, because many residents are not lovingly touched anymore. Not even the simple touch of a handshake, which many of them enjoyed for years in congregational life and attached so much belonging and identity, is available in the nursing home. Sad to say, they now find themselves completely without the benefit of the simple ritual of handshaking.

Shaking hands means that we are friends, we know each other, we trust each other, and we belong to the same body and embrace the same tradition. The pastor brings this reality to the nursing home in the act of handshaking. When the pastor shakes hands with a resident or a staff person in a nursing home, he or she says, "We belong to the same body, we are friends, we trust each other, and we are one." Handshaking is one of the few rituals that do not need words to be effective. In fact, sometimes words ruin the handshaking ritual, because the very act itself is more powerful and meaningful than any words can be, particularly in the nursing home.

The pastor may find that the handshaking ritual is prolonged for an extended period of time. It's the resident's way of saying, "I appreciate this and I don't get it very often, so I want to hold on to it for as long as I can." Sometimes I have held hands with residents for the entire visit, and they still did not want to let go when I got ready to leave. Sometimes the right hand is not available for handshaking (for any number of reasons), but the ritual, although it is often referred to as the "right hand of fellowship," is just as powerful when people extend their left hands. This ritual stands by itself. It requires no props, music, scripture, or anything else to make it effective. You, the pastor, should always be prepared to shake hands as often as you can with as many people as you can when you visit a nursing home.

The Lord's Supper

Other rituals like the Lord's Supper are very much appreciated as well. People remember what it means to commune, and often this ritual has been practiced on a level that is so deep and meaningful that dwindling mental alertness does not dull its effect. Any time is a good time to perform the ritual of the Lord's Supper.

Prayer

Not enough can be said about the ritual of prayer. However, one should not just assume that prayer covers everything or that a staff person, family member, or resident would automatically like to have prayer. Prayer is such a powerful tool that it should always be preceded by agreement on the part of those who will be involved in it. This may be achieved by simply asking, "Would you like a prayer?" or "May we pray?" If the person says no or has some resistance to prayer, it is a good idea to accept them where they are and not insist on the prayer.

Other Rituals

It is commonly believed that elderly people enter their childhood for a second time. To some degree, this may be true because many elderly people tend to be open to new and exciting things that they have never done before. One thing that children and elderly people have in common is that they are looking for practical solutions to issues they face *each day*. They are not so concerned about what it looks and sounds like or who likes it and who doesn't like it; their greatest motivation is "Will it work or satisfy my need?" This opens the door to creativity and innovation; the pastor has an opportunity to initiate new and meaningful rituals for residents and family members that are designed especially for the situations in which these persons find themselves. Some examples of creating new rituals are as follows:

One resident I used to visit had access to a lot of reading material (and had the time to read it). She made it her business to cut out certain things she thought would be interesting to me and helpful in my ministry. Some of them were, but what was more helpful to me than the articles themselves was the fact that she took the time and interest to cut them out for me. This became a ritual between us. Whenever I came to see her, she had saved certain articles for me to take with me when I left. Of course, she had to tell me why she chose certain articles and why she thought they would be helpful to me. This became a ritualistic way of beginning our time together.

Another resident I used to visit had lost her eyesight almost completely. She could read only with extreme difficulty and a lot of help from a very thick magnifying glass. She had read a lot in her lifetime and appreciated good books. The ritual we had between us was that whenever I came, I had to read for her, not just from the Bible, but also from whatever book or magazine that she happened to have. She seemed to have an inexhaustible supply of poetry and anecdotes. The amazing thing about this woman was that she could remember what she had available, direct me to a certain book, turn to a certain page, and read a certain poem or article. Not only could she remember the right place, but she could also remember the content of what I was reading. If I said a word wrong (which I often do when I read aloud), she would immediately correct me, like a schoolteacher might. I learned to be on my p's and q's when I was reading for her, or I would be embarrassed by her correcting voice. I used to think to myself, "Since you know this passage by heart, why don't you just rehearse it to yourself instead of having someone read it for you?" It was some time before I realized the value of our ritual: it was not that she could not recite certain scriptures and poems to herself; it was important to her that the pastor read them to her. She would tell her family that the pastor had come and read certain things to her. It was hearing the pastor's voice and having the pastor read from the source she supplied. And with her excellent memory she had the advantage of knowing that the pastor had not only read it well but also read it right.

I have never had this kind of ritual with a resident in a nursing home; however, another pastor said he had this ritual that he shared with a resident in a nursing home, and he shared it with me. This ritual had to do with eating. Every time he went to the nursing home to see her, he had to take something that they could eat together. Sometimes it was fruit, sometimes it was candy, sometimes it was baked goods, and sometimes it was peanuts (this just happened to be a person who still had teeth and could eat peanuts). A part of their visit was whatever they were eating together and like a movie when the credits come on when whatever they were eating was finished, it was time for him to leave. A student shared with me that one resident always required her to verify whatever she had read or heard on the news in between visits. The resident would not believe anything she had seen or heard happening in the community until the student had come and verified it. Needless to say, the resident had more time to keep up with the news events than the student did, so sometimes the student had to admit that she could not verify what was going on. The resident learned to handle this disappointment by accepting that at least you verified this, that and the other.

A man who happened to be a minister visited his aunt in the nursing home. He enjoyed photography and had a ritual with his aunt. Each time he went to visit her, he brought new pictures that he had taken of the family, the church, and special events. Sometimes he took pictures of her and the other residents in the nursing home and brought them back when he returned the next time. I don't remember how this ritual got started, but it was something that she looked forward to and that he enjoyed doing very much. Another person told me about working a puzzle with someone in a nursing home. It was something that they did together as a ritual; the puzzle would stand idle until he came to visit the resident. While he was there, they would put all the pieces together as a team. It was interesting how putting the puzzle together symbolized their efforts to put things together in her life. They both looked forward to spending time together on this activity.

Some might question how can these and other things you do with residents be rituals, especially of a pastoral nature. It is helpful to understand that rituals develop out of need. They were not all handed down from God. Rituals continue to be important in our lives because they give us structure in our relationships. After they are learned through repetition, they allow us the freedom to enjoy the meaning, rather than trying to remember what to do. Regardless of what is going on in our lives, they allow certain kinds of responses (hopeful and productive responses) and give meaning and identity to certain relationships that we enjoy. The pastor's presence is the greatest gift that he or she can share with the resident. Whatever is going on during that period of presence serves only to heighten and enrich the gift of presence. Whenever the pastor is present with the resident, it symbolizes and indeed manifests the presence of God to the resident. There is no ritual known to humankind that can do more than this.

DILEMMAS

One rule of thumb in pastoring is that people are capable of conducting their own lives. The corollary is that it is usually best to let people decide what is best for themselves. However, with elderly people some of this independence is lost, and decisions must be made on their behalf. It is a tremendous dilemma for a pastor when a family member says, "What should I do about my elderly loved one?" Sometimes a certain surgery has been recommended, a certain treatment has been suggested, or perhaps a family member is saying, "I have a great career opportunity, but it will mean moving away and leaving my loved one some distance away from where I will be." I am not aware of any rule of thumb that will help a pastor answer these and many other questions that are posed, because there is no obvious answer. This is one place where I truly believe the situation must be approached through a process of prayer and soul-searching. This is also where having a strong pastoral relationship is crucial. My own faith tells me that there is an answer to every question, and I also believe that God has a way to make everything work out for the best for those who love God.

Sometimes finding the right answer or solution to a dilemma requires a lot of searching. This is what we do as ministers: we look for spiritual needles in the haystacks of America. We are called upon to make sense of the unfashionable, the uncomfortable, and the unlovely. Few people really expect us to be greater and wiser than we really are. Most of all, God does not expect us to be all-knowing when these dilemmas arrive. What is expected of us is faithfulness. We must not run away and be afraid to come back to make the hard decisions; we must not defer those decisions to somebody else who might not care as much. We must not say, "It is too hard for me," "It's beyond me," or "It's not my business." It *is* our business. Our business is to be faithful in love and relationship—to be faithful in our presence and caring. It is our business to be the high priest, as it were, who stands between the confusion and challenge of the world and a powerful and loving God who has put us where we are, most likely for this very time and situation. It is our business to be faithful until the decision is made and the dilemma is resolved.

One thing I have found out about searching for answers to dilemmas is that sometimes the answer is in the searching. It is the process of faithfully searching that turns out to be the answer that we were seeking. I once had a student who spent a lot of time trying to find a scripture for a patient in the hospital. He never found it, but the patient was overjoyed that he spent so much of his time with her looking for it. In comparison to the time spent together, the scripture paled in importance and satisfaction. The student's peer group said there was no such scripture in the Bible and that the patient just did not want him to leave. In any case, it was a good thing that he was faithful to her need.

As we continue to develop pastoral relationships with staff persons, they will ask us to minister to other persons that we may not even know in the nursing home. Staff persons always have residents that they favor, are concerned about, and take care of as best they can. When they know that these residents are in need of pastoral care, they will steer any pastor they can in the direction of the resident. Most of the time, when this kind of referral is made, it always turns out to be more than what it seems like on the surface. The dilemma is, do I have time to get involved in another situation? Time is always a dilemma for the pastor. There are several things that I will say to a pastor struggling with the dilemma of time:

(1) The pastor needs to reexamine his or her call to ministry. Where do you see your calling? Perhaps it is the person in the nursing home that you do not believe you have time to serve. If you have ever felt that you understood your calling in the past, this may be a time to reexamine that calling and see if you are really where you are supposed to be and where God wants you to be. Perhaps this is a person that needs the reassurance that God has not forgotten him or her. Is this part of what it means to be a pastor?

(2) Every pastor needs to learn how to say no. This is difficult for some pastors. We often build ourselves up to a point where we can say no appropriately, but it is so easy to drift back into the deep pit of never saying no to anybody. In ministry it is just as important to know when to say no as it is to say yes. You cannot know when to say no unless you examine your identity as a pastor. It is how we see ourselves and how we see our ministry that tells us when we must say no.

To fulfill the request of a staff person in a nursing home to visit a resident may not be when we should say no. But we will never have enough time to fulfill that request if we do not learn how to say no to some other things. So saying no to some other inappropriate things that may not be ours to do may give us the necessary time to say yes when we are needed in the nursing home.

When I was teaching CPE in a hospital some years ago, a practice began among some of the other supervisors of giving the students only as much territory as they had time to handle. I rejected this practice and continued to give my students more than I knew they could do. I had one thought in mind: to help them learn how to say no. If students have only as many patients as they can comfortably visit, they will never have to deal with the dilemma of saying no. Because I assigned them more than they could possibly handle, they constantly had to prioritize where they spent their time and how much time they spent in whatever they were doing. The general pattern was usually that first they would stay late, then take stuff home, ask for help, or come back on their time off. Over a period of time, they began to struggle with the dilemma of not being able to do everything for everybody. At least annually, pastors should review where they are with this issue, because it is very important to their ministry. It is very interesting how our work in the nursing home can influence our entire ministry.

RESOURCES

The pastor will most often not find very many resources available in the nursing homes because caring for elderly people and making sure they have all of their needs being taken care of require nursing homes to prioritize their spending. (Nursing homes have to say no too.) Consequently, you may not find available communion sets or chapels, and you may even find it difficult to use the telephone, especially with any degree of privacy. It's very different from a hospital, where pastors are anticipated and resources are made available to them. However, while resources may be limited, access to the residents will be far greater, and, for example, parking is less of a problem.

Pastors, however, do have access to some resources *that nursing homes need.* Clothing is always an issue in the nursing home, as is soap, deodorant, toothpaste, and shaving materials. Many of these things are necessary for a sense of well-being, but are not essential to survival. Many of the residents in nursing homes have no family members or friends to provide these items for them, and it is difficult for the nursing home to always have them at hand. Pastors have access to congregations and persons within their membership who are looking for opportunities to make a difference in somebody's life. Here again, pastors can be effective bridges between the faith community and the needs of the larger community. The best way to handle helping nursing homes with supplies is to talk to the administrator.

Other resources that pastors have at their disposal are those persons who are willing to arrange worship services in the nursing home for residents. Nursing homes love to have a long list of persons and faith communities coming through on a routine basis to provide worship opportunities for residents and personnel as well. This does not mean that there are no worship opportunities available for personnel in nursing homes; some nursing homes schedule worship on a regular basis. However, it is much more meaningful to the residents when a group comes from outside to participate with them: It gives them additional community and shows them that they are still part of a living tradition. Seeing young people carrying on the traditions is a thrilling experience for them.

Nothing excites older people in nursing homes more than children. If children show up at the nursing home for no other reason than to just go around and talk or shake hands with people or read to them, the elderly people usually appreciate them very much. Having the children there is like having their own children and grandchildren there vicariously. Some teenagers who have visited nursing homes have reported having exciting and fulfilling experiences relating to elderly people. It amazes me sometimes that churches that are looking for ways to do meaningful things with young people in the church never think about taking them to a nursing home.

Many people believe they do not know what to say or how to act in a nursing home. In the nursing home setting if you say absolutely nothing at all you will be saying the right thing 90 percent of the time. If you do absolutely nothing at all, just the fact that you are there means that you have done a lot. No pastor, regardless of how good he or she may be in ministry, can do as much for residents and staff in a nursing home as a group of people who go in together. Sometimes the greater gift of ministry is not what we do, but what we cause to happen.

FIVE

IN THE FUNERAL HOME

Funeral homes came into existence to help provide for what historically took place in the family home. Before funeral homes, when there was a death in the family, the body of the deceased was cleaned and dressed by family members, laid out at home, often eulogized in the home after a period of viewing (what is often called a *wake*), and finally buried in the cemetery by family members. As families began to move away from agricultural life, became more mobile, and spread out all over the country, there were fewer and fewer family members available at times of death to take care of details. It was also natural that funeral homes began to make themselves available to provide services that used to happen in the homes of the deceased; at times, it seemed that funeral directors squeezed themselves in between the family and the pastor of the family. This was much more pronounced in some places than in others. For example, this practice was much more prevalent in urban areas than in rural areas; it was also practiced more in the North than in the South. Today, there is much more cooperation between pastors and funeral directors.

Today the funeral home and the funeral home director have a definite place and role to play at times of death and funerals. Funeral directors do more than direct funerals and burials. They are somewhat like hubs that are connected by spokes to a lot of different entities. For example, they are connected to the hospital; when someone dies, it is the funeral director who picks up the body. The funeral director is connected to the coroner's office. When there has been a death that may have occurred by unnatural causes, the funeral director works directly with the coroner. The coroner then makes a decision whether or not to do an autopsy. Once that decision is made, or after the autopsy is done, the coroner releases the body to the funeral director, who begins the embalming process. The funeral director is connected to the health department; there are certain laws and ordinances that govern how bodies are to be treated and buried. Sometimes a funeral director is connected to universities that receive bodies for research. The funeral director is connected to the family, of course, and also to the church, coordinating the preparation for the final celebration of the deceased person's life. Finally, the funeral director is connected to the cemetery, which receives the body for burial in its final resting place. Families rarely are aware of these procedures at all; it is the funeral director who is licensed to be sure that proper care is taken.

Funeral directors are natural partners for pastors. The pastor and the funeral director both have a relationship of trust with the family and share the same overall goal and similar responsibility of care during the funeral and burial. It is to everybody's advantage that the pastor and the funeral director have a good professional relationship. Most funeral home directors understand that their business is at least 50 percent relational regardless of what other services they may offer. Consequently, most of the time it is easy to develop relationships with funeral directors.

Many funeral homes offer "one-stop shopping" for families near or at the time of death. The people with whom the family deals are called bereavement consultants; they generally meet with families before death occurs or when death is anticipated. They share all of the options that are available at the time of death. In some situations the funeral home is located in the cemetery, so the family only has to go to one place for all of the services. This new approach to funerals has changed the entire process of caring for the dying in some cities and put some funeral home operators out of business.

A person may now go to a funeral home and make arrangements for funeral and burial services years before his or her death. The service may be paid for in advance with a guarantee that the service will be carried out in the way the person chooses. Even if the funeral home goes out of business, the prefuneral arrangements are guaranteed through a funeral home association. If one prefers to dispose of the body by cremation, that can be arranged and coupled with a memorial service.

Establishing a Pastoral Relationship with the Funeral Director

The profession of the funeral director is lonely. The funeral director cannot discuss his or her work with the average person. In spite of the fact that the funeral director performs a needed service, the work is still considered morbid, scary, and dirty. I have talked to many funeral directors in my career and have found that they are somewhat like ministers, because they are so busy doing their work they do not take a lot of time to be supportive of each other. In my personal experience with funeral directors, I find them eager to talk and tell stories about their work. I enjoy listening to them. They caution me from time to time, however, that these are stories they don't often get to tell. Not even pastors are willing to listen to their stories much of the time. Their stories include more than the services they render; the ones that I love so have to do with family dynamics. It will amaze you to know the kinds of family dynamics that funeral directors find themselves in the middle of. They certainly do not ask or want to be there, but they are the one professional person that some families have established a relationship with. At this juncture families often call them with all kinds of issues irrelevant to the funeral. The issues often involve fighting over the inheritance, who is the next of kin, who gets to sit where, who is responsible for the food, who is related how, and just keeping some semblance of peace in the family until they can muddle through the funeral.

After having managed the funeral so well, funeral directors are the natural choice for families to call upon to discuss other issues: How do I invest the money that I receive from the insurance? What should I do about the property that I am responsible for dividing? Is it okay to start dating again after two or three months? How do I deal with my siblings and other relatives who are angry with me and causing me grief? What about putting the parent that is left in a nursing home?

Some years ago I stopped driving to the cemetery after performing the funeral service. I make it known to the funeral director that I need transportation to and from the cemetery. Most of the time this means riding in the hearse along with the body, but this doesn't bother me. Those drives to and from the cemetery often give me an opportunity to deepen my rapport with the funeral director, because the funeral director rides in the hearse too. Of course we have an established relationship before the funeral, just to make sure that we are able to work together and understand each other's cues. This is what I call a professional relationship. We simply agree to cooperate to get a task done. The real rapport that will last for many years to come for all future funerals with that funeral director is the rapport that is established in the hearse between the cemetery and the funeral home or the church. I only have to ask two or three questions to "prime the pump," and then I just listen: How is business? How long have you been in this business? Do you still find it interesting? How do you take care of yourself? The last time I asked a funeral director how long he had been in this business, I hardly got to say another word. He told me things that he said he had never shared with anybody else. When we got back to the funeral home, he thanked me profusely for listening to him and letting him talk.

Funeral directors do their part to establish rapport as well. They usually tell me what a great eulogy I gave, even though I sometimes know better. They find other ways to compliment me and I like it, even if it is not true. They offer to help any way they can. They give me the same courtesy and service when they drive me to the cemetery as they give to the family. I realize part of this is because they want me to recommend another family to them; another part is because they have been doing it so long, it is just second nature. But, in spite of it all, I can tell that there is some true give and take between us. The director can help me do some genuine catharsis when I may need it, and my grief is made easier by the friendship he or she offers.

FUNERAL HOME STAFF

The funeral home staff will usually follow the lead of the funeral director where the pastor is concerned. If the pastor and the funeral director develop a good relationship, the funeral home staff will very likely learn to appreciate that pastor as well. It is a good thing to have open relationships with all of the staff, because each staff member sees family members in a different way. Each staff member relates to people differently and consequently learns things from family members that another staff person may not. Sometimes sharing this information with a parishioner's pastor may be of immense value in the pastor's efforts to continue support for that family member in the future. When the staff (of any institution) has a good relationship with the pastor, they often treat the pastor's parishioners with more kindness and courtesy.

Quite recently I talked to a parishioner's son. He was telling me about what his mother was going through in the hospital and how complex and confusing it all was for him. He made a point of telling me that it was the nursing assistant who really answered all of his questions and put him at ease. Several times he referred to her and said that had it not been for her, he did not know how he would be able to handle things. (This is an example of having a staff person taking special interest in this parishioner because of her relationship with the parishioner's pastor.) Staff persons are much like the funeral director; they do not have a lot of people they can talk to about what they do and are going through. If a pastor is willing to listen to them, he or she can develop and sustain a very helpful relationship.

RELATING TO THE FAMILY AND EXTENDED FAMILY

If you feel like you are on trial during the time of death, funeral, and burial, it is probably because you are. No matter how well you do other parts of your ministry, if you do poorly with the funeral, for some families all else you have done is for naught. Funerals are highly charged with emotion; that is simply the order of the day. Anger, fear, guilt, and shame run rampant at this time. Much of what people are experiencing emotionally is totally irrational, so the facts do not really make a lot of difference. For most people, a death in the family is going to be an emotional roller coaster, and there is very little you can do about it. Even the families that are quiet and/or stoic can leave you wondering and fearful of when the other shoe is going to drop.

There are some things that pastors need to do to come through these kinds of experiences with the least amount of pain and anguish:

(1) Teach your congregation what steps they need to take in the event of a death of a congregant. Do not wait until there is a death in a family; there should be a list of things to do that is available to families long before they experience the surprise or inevitability of someone dying in their family. It should tell them what to do and who to contact.

(2) In a death situation the pastor must keep in mind who has priority in receiving pastoral care. Is it the family that is left behind—the congregation, the visitors, the friends of the deceased, or the dignitaries who come to the funeral? Not everybody is going to be satisfied, regardless of what the pastor does. However, it is helpful for you to know where you need to focus your energies.

This may point a finger at a larger issue. What is the funeral all about anyway? Is it a celebration of the life of the person who died? Is it an attempt to make the loved ones feel comforted? Is it an opportunity to do evangelism? Is it an occasion to preach a great sermon? If the pastor has not answered these questions, it will be difficult for him or her to know how to focus his or her ministry. The question is different in each situation, so, therefore, because the pastor answered it well the last time does not mean that the same answer will apply this time. Some pastors simply focus on whatever will get them the largest donation to the church or their own pocket. To this I can say it certainly raises a question of authenticity, professional ethics, and just plain old good judgment. A successful funeral, as far as a pastor is concerned, is doing the right thing for the right reason. The pastor usually can live with whatever happens as a result of doing the right thing for the right reason.

(3) As I stated earlier, emotions rule the day in this setting. A wise pastor who understands this will be sure not to add "oxygen" to the flame. Because there are so many emotions going around, the pastor should be certain that he or she stays away from unnecessary issues that could create more stress and strain on the family. The best way to accomplish this is to be compassionate to all, regardless of their relationship and/or role. Somebody has to be rational. Somebody has to be calm; somebody has to be looking beyond the present moment at what the results of emotions getting out of hand will mean for many years to come. This is not a time for a pastor to join sides, become judgmental, criticize, or even tell inappropriate jokes. This is a time for the pastor to be solemn, prayerful, relational, and consistent but compassionate in every way.

(4) The pastor should take the theological high road. What do I mean by this? The pastor should use all of his or her power, influence, and authority to be sure that the funeral is conducted in a worshipful, spiritual, and sacred way. The pastor should not allow the funeral to fall into becoming a show, finger-pointing or blaming session, or an opportunity for persons to stand in the limelight. A funeral is the one place where there should always be dignity in its character and meaning in its execution. That is not to say that stories cannot be told and that humor should not be enjoyed, but the pastor should be careful not to allow this worshipful experience to become a brawl. The loved one who died is somebody's parent, somebody's child, somebody's sibling, or somebody's spouse. Loved ones need to know that they celebrated the funeral service in a dignified way when they put their loved one away. It gives them comfort and eases their grief.

RELATING TO THE EXTENDED FAMILY

It is my experience with a number of families that at the time of death some extended family members do all they can to appear to be the closest person to the deceased. While it is true that there are no definite lines that separate family from extended family, pastors should be careful not to get caught up in the fray of family members jockeying for a more favored position. I spoke earlier about each family having a leader. The pastor is very wise to identify the leader of any family that he or she is relating with, particularly at the time of death and the funeral. However you do it, know who the real leader of the family is. Once you know the leader of the family, you can relate with the family through the leader. It is the family's responsibility to decide who is extended family and who is not. It is the family's responsibility to maintain itself. All outsiders, including the pastor, are asking to get chewed up when they get in the middle of family strife. Work with the leader of the family to accomplish the goals and desires of the family.

Regardless of where a pastor may focus his or her ministry, ultimately the pastor is responsible for the entire family, relatives, friends, and the congregation. This is another reason why the pastor should stay above the fray and function at a high theological position when dealing with death and the funeral. By this, I mean in God's sight we are all sinners and need God's grace. We are all God's children and are all loved by God. It is God's desire that each of us love and honor God in all things and love each other as we love ourselves. This is the highest level of theology: love of God and neighbor. At a lower level, there may be a tug-of-war. At a high theological level, everything comes together into a synergy for all people of faith and for many who are not of the faith.

As soon as I mention people of faith, I must also say that there are people attending funerals who are not people of faith. I also need to say that the pastor is responsible for them as well. The pastor needs to respond to the family, the friends, the saved, the unsaved, and anybody else who shows up or hears about the service, whether or not he or she sees God in this situation. Part of our responsibility as pastors is to help people see God in all situations.

What is God saying? What is God doing? What would God like to see happen as a result of this whole situation? After all, whoever we are, we have come from God, and to God we return. No one gives birth to himself or herself. And even if we returned only to the earth from which we came, and that is the extent of our faith, we are still returning to the Creator of the earth. One might say that, as much as any time in a pastor's ministry, at a funeral he or she is a true prophet of God. If life itself is sacred, then death is holy. This is particularly true for those who have spent their lives well, investing their faith in a religious lifestyle and in the God of the universe. They deserve to be lifted up in the finale of their earthly existence.

When I was the assistant pastor of a congregation and literally in charge after the death of the senior pastor, an elderly person in the congregation died. This woman had no immediate relatives in the area. In due time a distant niece and a more distant cousin showed up to claim the body and make funeral arrangements. The first thing they did was to decide that the funeral would not be held at the church, but at the funeral home. Our church was a large congregation, and the woman who died was held in high regard. The decision not to hold the funeral at the church meant that many people would not be able to attend the service, because they would not all fit into the small funeral home.

In addition, the family made some other changes in the program that had been previously requested by the deceased parishioner. I was not included in any part of the arrangements; the funeral director had contacted another assistant pastor of the church, who then allowed all of these changes to be made. When I arrived at the funeral home and realized what was going on, I talked to the funeral director, with whom I fortunately had a good relationship. He explained that this family had been highly agitated and controlling; they had asked that the site of the funeral be moved, because they did not see a funeral as a religious matter. I said to the funeral director, "This woman who died was a member of our church. She cast her lot with Christ and the church and with God. These church people who have come to her funeral today *are* her family. They have come to celebrate her homegoing. Neither she nor her congregation will be denied what they expect and need at this funeral."

After a song that had little meaning to anybody attending the funeral, I stepped to the podium. I had prayed that I would have the courage to be a prophet in this situation. I had also prayed that I would be guided by the Holy Spirit to take the theological high road and show compassion for the benefit of those who were in pain and for the benefit of the woman who had served so faithfully until she died. I had compassion also for the family members who seemed to have little appreciation for the faith of their relative. I spoke much in the same way I did to the funeral director, except with much more authority. I apologized to everyone that the celebration plans had been changed from what we had anticipated and expected. I apologized that I was not available to be certain that we would have the funeral at the church, where we would have been more comfortable. I assured them that we would make the best of the situation as it was, and that we had come to celebrate, and celebrate we would.

I acknowledged the right of the extended family to make some decisions about how things needed to be done. However, I lifted up the theological concept of community. The deceased woman was a part of our community. The community owes something to her and to itself. We are a community of faith and a community of God. We must not deny who we are and whose we are, especially at this time and at this event in our history. With that, I took charge and redirected the celebration so that it became what I felt it should have been in the beginning. At the end I had the opportunity to speak with the extended family members who had come to town and changed everything. They were grateful that I had taken charge and lifted up their loved one to a higher level than they had seen fit to do. The congregation was grateful because they had a chance to say good-bye in the way that they wanted to and had done so many times for others who had died. The funeral director was relieved that everything had worked out well and that people had not had a bad experience at his funeral home. I was thankful that God had chosen to use me instead of someone else to manifest the words of the Scriptures: "I will never leave you nor forsake you" (Heb. 13:5 NKJV).

Pastors cannot always take charge as I did at that particular funeral. However, pastors should be aware of opportunities to guide people to a higher level of spirituality and theology soundness when family members, especially extended family members, are making decisions that lead to a funeral not in keeping with what the deceased person would have wanted. It may be well to remember that other parishioners are watching and wondering what if it were them and their family members were standing in the way of them having the best send-off as they would like. The other thing to remember is that family members are not experts, to say the least, in what needs to be done at a funeral. When they are grieving, they are even less capable of making judgments about these matters. I believe the family members in the story above did not intend to do any harm, but they just did not know how to do what needed to be done.

RELATING TO FRIENDS

We live in a time when some people's lives are lived in such a way that they may have friends who are closer to them than their family members are. It is not uncommon for me to hear people make the statement, "I chose my friends but with my family I had no choice at all." Even though friends may have been closer to the deceased and may have known him or her better than the family, they have no legal standing when it comes to the funeral and burial. However, the pastor must respect that they did have a close relationship with the parishioner who died. If the family accepts the friends, it makes the situation much easier. However, in these kinds of situations the family often resents the friends and does not want them to be anywhere around. Sometimes there is a lot of history to these feelings that may or may not be valid, but often the feelings exist even when there is no long history. This raises again the questions I listed earlier about to whom the pastor is responsible and where he or she needs to focus his or her ministry. The real answer to these questions is that the pastor is to some degree responsible for all of them, family and friends.

Another approach to take with family and friends is the same approach that is taken legally and ethically in regard to other issues that come up when a person dies. The bottom line is that the life of a person belongs to that person. What happens to that person after death should be determined by the person himself or herself, if at all possible. Since he or she cannot speak for himself or herself after death, it is necessary to determine from what is known of the person's character, wishes, attitude, and so on, what that person would like to have done in the present situation. In the case where an individual has chosen his or her friends over his or her family, it must be accepted that if he or she chose these friends in life, it would seem to indicate that this would be the choice in death. If the individual lived in two different communities and related to them on an equal basis, that would indicate that the individual would desire that both communities be respected at his or her death.

Sometimes family members and friends will surrender their determination in favor of what they believe the one they loved would desire at the present time. The pastor's responsibility is to raise the issue for them to reflect upon. The pastor may also be able to offer a creative way for both factions to have their needs met. For example, one faction could furnish a solo while the other makes a statement or reads a paper or poem. It is not uncommon that some people lived in more than one community, and they are just as comfortable in one as they are in another. If those communities really care, they will do all they can to bring honor to the name and personhood of the one who died.

Finally, the pastor may take the theological approach. What would God want to happen at this time? Who would God accept and who would God reject? Would God find a way to satisfy all concerned or not? The ultimate question for the pastor is what does God expect of him or her at this time in this situation? When it comes to a funeral and their friends who have no legal standing are not welcomed by the family, it raises the question of whether a funeral should be conducted based on the love of law or the law of love. Faith says the latter.

THE PASTOR'S ROLE AND AUTHORITY

I have identified the pastor's role and authority earlier by the questions I raised. The pastor has to decide whom he or she is serving in doing a funeral: God or humanity. This helps him or her come to grips with the ultimate purpose of a funeral. Because death remains a universal experience and because of God's prerogative to act any time and in any way God chooses, most of the time the pastor, as God's representative, will have authority in a funeral situation. The question is usually not how much authority does the pastor have, but does the pastor know what to do with that authority?

For example, some pastors have a policy in their churches that they will not do an open-coffin funeral. By that, I mean the coffin must be closed before the service, especially the eulogy, and cannot be opened again. The reason is that the pastor does not want what he or she is saying in the eulogy to be overshadowed by the crying and grieving of family members. This policy is tantamount to telling a family when and how they must grieve. If the funeral is for the family and for the celebration of the life of the one who died, such a rule would seem to be an abuse of the pastor's authority. I suggest that the pastor may be uncomfortable with the grieving family and is using such a rule to curtail the crying that may happen when family members see the body for the last time.

Some pastors refuse to ever conduct a funeral unless the deceased meets certain criteria that are set by the pastor, such as being a member in good standing. Sometimes the pastor will do the funeral but not allow it to take place in the church; it must happen at the funeral home. Because of the nature of funerals, the pastor has enough authority to make these policies stick, but it certainly raises serious questions of abuse of power. Sometimes families who have not thought twice about the church before will turn to the church because of the acceptance and care that they experience with the pastor at the time of their loved one's death. On the other side of the ledger, if a pastor abuses his or her power around the issue of a funeral, that pastor is likely to pay for that mistake in one way or another. The pastor needs to use his or her authority to bring peace and calm to the situation, rather than to stir up trouble. Remember, there are already enough emotions operating around this whole issue of death and burial, and when the pastor adds his or her own emotional baggage to the mix, it makes for a very difficult situation for everybody.

Last, there are still some pastors who take it upon themselves to judge the dead. They will even go so far as to say that the person's behavior is responsible for his or her death because God was punishing them. The judging of dead people is definitely the prerogative of God. Whenever a pastor takes it upon himself or herself to judge the living or the dead, he or she is misusing his or her pastoral authority. As the Scriptures say, "Who are you to judge another's servant? To his own master he stands or falls" (Romans 14:4*b* NKJV). God does not need any help in making righteous and holy judgments about anybody's life. Misusing authority is the most certain way of losing authority. A pastor's authority should be used only to protect, heal, and comfort those who are in pain and anguish due to the loss of a loved one. Any time a pastor uses his or her authority to further his or her own agenda, particularly at the time of a funeral, it is a misuse of authority and a sad commentary on that pastor's ministry.

RITUALS AND ETIQUETTE

When I'm teaching, preaching, or counseling, I see myself as a pastoral midwife. I bring nothing new to the table; my job is to help bring forth and give birth to those ideas, feelings, and greater awareness that is trying to be born. My task is to pave the way for what is coming. But when I am attending to a death, funeral, and/or burial, I am an angel of comfort. It is not my purpose to do teaching, prophesying, giving insight, or pointing out a truth (although all of these may happen) that has often escaped the awareness of the one who I am ministering to. I am simply trying to bring comfort to someone who has experienced a tremendous loss. That in itself is a ritual. It actually is the middle part of a ritual.

The Nature of a Ritual

A ritual in its completeness has three parts: The first stage is "separation and death" of the entire state of a person. This stage of a ritual is total loss of all that gives a person identity and authority. It is total devastation of everything that the person has been and sees himself or herself as being. The loss of a loved one is a perfect manifestation of the first stage of a ritual. It reduces the loved one who is left to a powerless sense of self and a confused state of being. I can hardly think of anything that is more devastating than to lose someone you love very dearly to death.

The second stage is a limbo period in time and space. Space and time are now different and yet not what they are going to be.

It is the fragile stage of transition and transformation. Regardless of who the persons were before they entered into this ritual, what they will become will be determined in large measure by what happens in this second stage. During the second stage, the pastor is the teacher, the guide, the supporter, and the comforter. The pastor is the one with the authority, the one who is strong, the one who is in touch with reality, not only of the present, but also of the future. He or she is the one who cares.

All of the family members, friends, congregation, and so on, are part of the pastor's care during the second caring stage of this ritual. They have all come from different places and different states of being, but they are now all in the same place with the primary goal of simply having the hope of being in a better place when the second stage is ended. During the second stage the parishioners are so vulnerable that the pastor must take care not to wound or frighten them. It is most important that the pastor handle all who are in or under his or her care with tenderness and love. This is one time that the pastor does not have the fear of being too nice, loving too much, or not holding persons accountable. The family and friends, and the congregation as well, need from the pastor nothing but love, love, and more love.

The third stage of the ritual is the reentry stage as the new person one has become. In the first stage one is totally separated, in the third stage one has been reaggregated, but the difference is that the reaggregated one is not the same person that was separated. When the person was separated, he or she was complete and whole in whatever state they were. In the third stage when one reenters society, that person is like a new baby becoming whole again. The third stage will take a long time and be punctuated by new insights and new feelings about oneself and the new world in which he or she finds himself or herself.

DILEMMAS

Just as a pastor gets it all figured out and knows how to relate to funeral staff and directors, families, friends, congregants, and whomever, another dynamic is added to the mix. It is the dynamic of various dilemmas that arise as a result of abnormal death situations. Abnormal death has to do with those situations that occur as a result of an accident, violence, house fire, suicide, sudden infant death syndrome, or a death of a child. Even when a person lives to a ripe old age of ninety-something or more and dies in his or her sleep, loved ones still have difficulty letting the person go and accepting his or her death. It's extremely painful when a person who has a serious illness for many years and suffered tremendous agony through many treatments and efforts to sustain his or her life finally dies.

There was a woman who worked for forty-something years as an administrator and assistant to the president of a hospital. When she was required to retire at seventy (only because it was the policy), she left that institution and went to another institution for twenty-three years. Word was that she never missed a day at work or ever had a sick day in her life. At ninety-three she retired from her second career and shortly thereafter she contracted leukemia. When she came to the hospital and was diagnosed with leukemia, she became very angry and said it was not fair. For many people it is never fair to be ill and to die at any age. The one comforting thought of dying at a ripe old age is that at least the person lived a full life. Many people have used that phrase when talking about their loved ones having died, but if something happens that cuts that full life to a shorter life, therein lies a dynamic that is really difficult for many people to deal with. The pastor who is providing care in this situation will most definitely have his or her hands full.

I live in Detroit now, where this year alone twenty-six people under the age of sixteen have died violently. Some of the children who died were sleeping in their beds and killed by stray bullets shot into the house. Last year five small children died in one fire. Recently a mother left her three-year-old and ten-month-old children in the car on a hot summer day while she went to get her hair done. They died a horrible death. I once counseled with a woman who was very close to her sister. Her sister was apparently a victim of a murder suicide perpetrated by her brother-in-law.

When she arrived at the home where her sister and her husband were dead, the police said the scene was too horrid for her to see. Because they did not let her see her sister at that time, three years later she had not really accepted her sister's death.

When a person dies while sleeping or even from a horrible disease, the loved ones can accept that it was the natural order of things. What happens in violence, suicide, and infant death, the natural order of things is disrupted and tampered with. Many parents whose children have died have said to me, "The child is not supposed to die before the parent." What they are really saying is there is a natural order that's painful enough in itself: but when something unnatural takes place, there is no basis on which to accept that reality. The grief and loss that a person must endure when a death has occurred due to unnatural causes is not just the death alone or the loss of the one they loved; it is the loss of security that they felt they had in the natural order of things. How does one grieve the loss of security, the changing of the rules, the eradication of the boundaries that once was his or her world? If children can die before their parents, if people can take their own life without anybody seeing the symptoms beforehand, if a stray bullet can wipe out any member of the family at any time, if a safe driver can be killed in an auto accident, then what security do we have? This question adds powerful dynamics to any grief situation.

Another question that must be dealt with due to an unnatural death is the question of responsibility. Some people can never get past their own guilt because they assign to themselves some responsibility for the death of their loved one. In the case of suicide, they tell themselves they should have seen the signs that were present before the death occurred. They feel guilty because they did not get the child to the doctor sooner, even though the doctor says it would not have made any difference how soon the parent brought the child in. In the case of violent death, loved ones may feel guilty for not rearing their children in a better way, for not living in a different neighborhood, for allowing their loved one to drive the car that was involved in a accident, and so forth. It is amazing the lengths people will go to claim some responsibility for the death that occurs, especially when it is an unnatural death.

Some theorists believe it is important for loved ones to feel that they had some control of what happened to be able to go on with their lives. Accepting some responsibility makes them feel that they have some control. Imagine how it would feel not to have any control of anything at any time and that death is constantly stalking everyone you love. Even when loved ones bargain with God or other people, they still may assign guilt to themselves for not saying "I love you" every opportunity they had, for failing to kiss the last time they were with the person, for angry words they may have said shortly before the person died, or in some way failing to make that person's last moments of life as pleasant as they imagine they could have been if the survivor had done something different. It is true that family members blame the doctors, the drunk driver, the gang, the person who hanged himself or herself, or anyone who failed to prevent this death from occurring. But even while the loved one is pointing a finger at others to whom he or she assigns responsibility, three fingers on that same hand are pointing back at himself or herself. It is a difficult thing for some people to get past their own guilt about an unnatural death.

When the pastor comes on the scene, he or she brings another dynamic into the situation: our powerful and loving God. Where was God when this event took place? Why did God allow this to happen? Coupled with their own sense of grief and the lack of God having intervened, the question is often "Why is God punishing me?" The meaning that they make at this point in their grief is that God has not behaved fairly or lovingly. A lesser criticism may be that God has made a mistake. The ultimate question is based on the belief that there is a reasonable, rational, acceptable reason for what has occurred, but God is being very quiet about it and will not reveal the answer of why this has occurred.

In a natural death situation the presence of the minister (who is the incarnation of God and Christ) may be a very comforting thing for the family who has suffered a loss. In an unnatural death situation, the presence of the minister may be anything but a sense of comfort for the family members. How does a minister pray to God for someone who is angry with God? How does the pastor bring comforting words from the Scriptures to someone who has decided that Scriptures cannot be trusted? How can the pastor use the resources of the church, religious tradition, and the community of faith to bring hope, comfort, and resolution to someone who feels betrayed by all he or she has ever believed?

There are some things that we know do not help. I know of no special, secret, holy, or any other kind of words that will restore all that has been lost. These kinds of words may make the person feel better for the moment, but the pain of grief will certainly return. We never know how effective prayer can be in any situation; however, prayer alone does not resolve these kinds of situations and sometimes the persons involved are definitely opposed to having any kind of prayer on their behalf. To encourage people to leave it in God's hands and tell them that in time they will understand it better is another way of saying, "Continue in your denial of the whole situation." Finally, this is one situation that the pastor cannot do for the person involved; this is one time they have to do their own work.

I suppose there are some readers who are now asking the question "Then what does work?" The answer to that question is that sometimes nothing works. However, here are some things that have been helpful. In a situation involving an unnatural death, the loved ones' normal grief process has been thrown off track by the special dynamics created by the unnatural event. They not only have grieving to do; they also have issues that further complicate the grieving process. There is no way to predict how long it will take to help a person resolve the issues that surround an unnatural death; however, the following process may be used to work toward that goal: *content, dynamics,* and *meaning.*

Content

To move toward resolving the issue of the unnatural circumstances of the death of a loved one, persons need time and opportunity to talk about what is going on with them. They can only do this most effectively with someone with whom they have a good relationship, which is characterized by respect and trust with someone they know really cares for them like the pastor. The first level of the process is to talk about the content of the event: the facts; the details; the persons, places, times; and conclusions. It is important to keep in mind that the content of the situation will vary from person to person. Even though they all may have been apprised of the information, they may have been there when it happened, they may have participated in one way or another, but their perception of what happened is different. They need their own perceptions accepted, even though it may differ from the official report.

Sometimes when working with them as a group, they will be able to come to a consensus on various details and facts that are different among them. It is the group's responsibility to do that and not be led there by the pastor who is trying to help them. The pastor's role on a content level is to continue to ask for more information: What happened? Then what happened? Please continue, tell me more. The pastor's role is to encourage all of the content to come forth and accept it as it is stated. This does not mean that the pastor cannot ask for clarification. It is important to realize what you are accepting. But after asking for and receiving an explanation, the explanation must then be accepted too.

Dynamics

Dynamics are related to feelings and attitudes. At some point when the content is complete, the pastor must lead those he or she is trying to help in expressing how they feel about what happened. Feelings and attitudes go together. Attitudes represent the values people live by. When a value has been violated it motivates certain feelings. Other feelings are motivated simply from the event itself. A mixture of judgment and horror is often bottled up inside of the person and can fester for years if it is not allowed to come out. The pastor's role is to encourage these dynamics to be expressed. Needless to say, if the pastor has any judgment or shows any discomfort with any of the dynamics that are expressed, it will cut off the expression. The pastor must also remember that adding his or her feelings to the dynamics will simply add fuel to the fire. Just like vomiting up some harmful substance, when grieving persons vent these dynamics, they are ridding themselves of horrid, harmful energy that is doing and will continue to do damage to their psyche.

It has been my experience that when persons have carried emotional baggage around for a long time, part of the issue is the way the persons feel about themselves. To let go of the emotions feels like it would hurt or harm them. The truth is that it is just the opposite. What helps them to vent the emotions is trusting that they will still be accepted and valued. A woman's husband died suddenly; she was not able to grieve openly and unrestrained. After nearly two years she was still in the early stages of her grief. She went to a grief counselor and was able to say that she was angry with her husband, something she had forcefully denied before. Once she was told that that was understandable and normal, she was able to vent a lot of pent-up emotions. She talked about sometimes wishing her children were not there. The most important thing was her feelings of guilt that she had not done all she could to show her love during her late husband's life. When the counselor did not judge her for this, but instead suggested that it was time for her to forgive herself, she began to feel much better. The point here is that catharsis alone is not in itself healing, but acceptance (by the pastor) after pouring out their emotions.

In preparation for the final stage of this process, it is helpful for the pastor to help the person or persons focus on their dynamics. Such questions as "What about this whole event bothers you the most?" helps the person to narrow down to the dynamic that is most powerful and forceful for them. A similar question like "What is the part of this whole thing that you find most difficult to accept?" helps the person to move beyond the mass of dynamics to the more serious or problematic part of what is going on inside of them. This prepares them for the next stage of the process, which is *meaning*.

Meaning

Ultimately, to move toward resolving this situation (not the total grief but the complicating issues of the unnatural circumstances) the person must be able to make meaning of what has happened. Nobody can make meaning for the individual. This is something that one must do for oneself.

The pastor's role in helping the person or persons make meaning is simply to ask the question "How do you make meaning of all of this?" The meaning will be different for each individual and for the same individual at different times. It is important not to suggest meaning to anyone who is trying to make meaning, but to be patient while they struggle to find some meaning for themselves. They may ask the question "What does it mean to you?" but the appropriate response is "It is not important what it means to me, but what it means to you." Again, let me urge that the meaning is the individual's meaning and it may stand the pastor on his or her ear theologically. This is not the time to challenge a person's theology. The goal here is to help them resolve the issue of the unnatural circumstances of a death so that they can move on with their grief process. There may be plenty of time later for somebody to help them with their theology. As a matter of fact, when a person shares his or her meaning with a pastor at this point in the process, it is a precious and sacred gift that the person gives to the pastor. It should be received in that way and accepted as it is.

Finally, going through this process with a person may help him or her feel better for the moment. They may need to repeat the whole process several times before they can come to a resolution. I always encourage pastors to create support groups in their congregations where people with similar kinds of experiences can come and repeat this process with each other. How many times it will have to be repeated is a question that no one can answer. How well it will work for a particular individual is a question no one can answer. I will say only this: if a pastor is willing to give of himself or herself in relationship with a wounded person, that wounded person may be more open to receiving whatever pastoral care the pastor has to give through the ritual of funeral or prayer.

Even though a person may respond to the ministry offered through a funeral, that does not mean that the grief is over or that these same emotions will not be visited again and again. The first year and a half is the most crucial period of time for someone who is grieving. Many people are ready to move on by two to three years after the death. However, it is not unusual at all for persons to grieve for several years. There are many different reasons for this prolonged period of grief. It is difficult to move on until a person can make meaning of the death and make sense of the situation. These two dynamics are not the same thing, and it is difficult to say which one needs to come first.

Making meaning of the death is more of a spiritual process. It is the process of answering the question "Why did this happen?" After a lot of anger and finger pointing (including pointing at oneself), there is finally a recognition that things happen in this life, but God is still on the throne and still loves us all. Meaning making puts things back in order; it is a different order from before the death, but it is an order that allows the person to develop an emotional and spiritual routine again.

On the other hand, making sense of the situation responds to the question "What now, or what next?" This question is a rational question. It obviously needs to be answered again and again. The entire process of making meaning and making sense happened many, many times before a family would leave the hospital after a death when I was a chaplain. But it has to be done again the next day and the next week. Finally, with time, the meaning seems to be sufficient, the sense begins to be manageable, and the person moves on with life.

RESOURCES

Pastors should not expect themselves to have the knowledge of how to help all individuals work through these dynamics that occur in an unnatural death. The pastor should be alert for the opportunity to refer the person or persons to someone who specializes in the area of grief and bereavement. Pastors should always have within their network of professionals the name and number of someone they know and trust will do a good job in helping a person resolve these issues. If the person does not respond positively to the pastor early in the process, it probably means they need professional help to work through these issues. The sooner the pastor makes the referral, the better.

It would be wonderful if all of our funerals were for persons who died in their sleep at a very old age; however, in this society, that kind of death happens less frequently all the time. Anybody in ministry today will most likely be involved with someone who has experienced an unnatural death situation, and the pastor will have to find a way to help him or her bring resolution to his or her pain. An unnatural death throws a person off balance. Such a person needs all the support he or she can get. Since people going through such an experience are so fragile, the pastor can do some of his or her best ministry just holding hands or referring them to someone who can do that.

SIX

IN THE PASTOR'S OFFICE

T he term "counseling" is used to describe a great number of interactions that take place between people; indeed, there are many forms and levels of counseling. What happens between a pastor and the pastor's parishioners in the pastor's office is the level of counseling on which we will focus in this chapter. We will also look at the difference between in-depth counseling (long-term, dealing with deep-seated psychological and emotional issues) and pastoral care (short-term, dealing with responses to events in a parishioner's life) as well as some of the things that a pastor needs to know to be effective in the counseling that he or she does.

COUNSELING VERSUS CARE

The entire ministry that pastors do with their parishioners is pastoral care; even teaching and preaching are ways to care for congregants. Pastors have a general concern for the well-being of their parishioners, but sometimes a problem may be serious enough that it requires special care and attention or intervention. This intervention, which may necessitate several meetings with the pastor to get through it, is counseling. While counseling may take many forms and address a diverse list of subjects, it usually is characterized by a longer duration of time and energy than most pastoral care situations. One way to understand the difference between pastoral care and counseling is to consider the entire ministry with parishioners as pastoral care and counseling as extended pastoral care, or parish counseling.

PASTORAL COUNSELING

Time spent with a parishioner is one way to look at pastoral counseling; another aspect of it is the seriousness of the issues being raised. How serious it is may be determined by the effect that the problem has on the parishioner and other people. If the issue being raised is keeping the person from going to work every day, that may be more serious than having missed an appointment. The mention of divorce in a marriage is certainly more serious than a disagreement about occasionally eating something that is not on the diet. Most issues raised with the pastor are helped when the pastor listens carefully and helps the parishioner to interpret what has happened or is happening. If the situation needs much more serious attention than this, it may be something that should be referred. More will be said about referral later in this chapter.

Counseling issues can rarely be resolved in one session: however, it is not just the time or number of sessions that characterize counseling, but also the structure of the sessions. The pastor needs to work out an agreement with the parishioner when and where the sessions will take place. They also need to agree how long each session will be. If a fee will be involved, it needs to be settled up front. This agreement is a very important part of the process because it communicates mutual respect and availability for the persons involved.

Pastors need to remember that when they are seeing someone in their office several times, powerful dynamics are at work. The parishioners' guard is down, because they feel safe and cared for. Just the fact that the pastor took time to see them is powerful in itself. Many parishioners will idealize the pastor, meaning they will see the pastor as the most perfect and ideal person they have ever met. It is not unusual for parishioners to fall in love with the pastor during this extended period of pastoral care. The danger signs include trying to stay just a little longer when the session is completed, calling to talk to the pastor in between sessions, total compliance with everything the pastor suggests, bringing gifts to the pastor for no reason, giving the pastor a lot of compliments, wanting the pastor to make decisions for them, and hanging on every word that the pastor says. Astute pastors will know they have a problem themselves when they are eager to see the parishioners because it feels good to spend time with them and to help them. It is always important for pastors to be aware of their own feelings when counseling with a parishioner.

Sometimes the parishioner is on a committee or sings in a choir that has been problematic for the pastor. It may be difficult for the pastor or the parishioner to avoid feelings from other situations because of their work together. It is usually helpful to address this issue before it becomes a problem in the session. The pastors need to own up to their feelings of anger, disappointment, and frustration, and assure the parishioner that it will not influence the work they need to do about the parishioner's issues. Pastors should also request that the parishioner not let other feelings control this time with the pastor. Often good healing takes place in these sessions because the pastor and the parishioner can see each other differently than ever before. It does not have to be a long statement, but short and to the point: "We have not always seen eye to eye on some issues. I want you to know that my feelings about those issues will not be a part of these counseling sessions. I hope you will agree to put your other feelings aside as well, until we get through this issue."

ESTABLISHING A PASTORAL RELATIONSHIP

The process discussed in chapter 1 about establishing rapport is pertinent here in the pastor's office as well. It should be noted that regardless of the kind of relationship that a pastor may have with a parishioner prior to the parishioner's coming to the pastor's office for counseling, there may not be enough rapport between them to further the counseling process. Many pastors have casual relationships and sometimes even social relationships with their parishioners. They talk to them on Sunday after the sermon; they share stories with each other about family and other events on occasion; sometimes they've had the opportunity to work together on certain projects and have gotten to know each other fairly well.

When the parishioner comes to the pastor's office for counseling, regardless of the history of their relationship, this is new. This is new because the parishioner is not at his or her best. Seeing the pastor for counseling may be the last resort out of many things that the parishioner has tried. If an event has blindsided the parishioner, this may be the first place he or she has gone. Parishioners may fear that what they are about to tell the pastor may change how the pastor sees them and may destroy the good relationship that they have enjoyed for so long. This is a new experience because neither the pastor nor the parishioner knows what the outcome will be. But you can be fairly sure that the issues most likely involve other people, that the dynamics of the issues are at least somewhat exaggerated, and that the parishioner feels powerless to some degree. It is important that you focus on establishing rapport before moving on to the dynamics that have brought the parishioner to your office.

Recently a pastor friend of mine referred one of his favorite parishioners to me for counseling. We had never met before she came to my office, even though she knew who I was. The pastor had shared very little with me about what was going on, but I knew enough to know that she was in terrible agony. When she walked in and sat down, I asked her about how difficult it was for her to find her way to my office. Fortunately, her brother had brought her to the session, and between the two of them they had no difficulty finding it. I affirmed her on how well they had followed my directions and their instincts to find their way with no problems. I began to talk to her about where she was from, where she was born, and where she was reared. She was almost in tears when she sat down. But when I began to ask about her family life, she perked up immediately. She was a delightful person to talk with, and in a few minutes we were laughing and talking about some of her family stories.

I make it my business to always see clients that my pastor friends refer to me, but this pastor had said that this was one of his favorite parishioners and I took special care of her. I took my time and enjoyed establishing rapport with her. After fifteen or twenty minutes we were like old friends who had known each for a long time. It was then, and only then, that I asked her why she had come to see me. As she reached for the Kleenex that I always keep handy when I am seeing clients, I knew that I had done the right thing in taking time to establish a rapport with her. Even with a good rapport, it was difficult for her to tell her story. Not only did the good rapport I established put her at ease, but it also gave me enough information about her that I was in a better position to assess the dynamics that she shared.

THE PASTOR'S OFFICE

The pastor's office should be a place of sanctuary. People who go to the pastor's office should feel that it is a place of safety, honesty, integrity, and ethical behavior. If the parishioner is uncomfortable in the pastor's office, the counseling process will not work well. This is not to say that the parishioner will not be anxious at the onset of counseling; most people are anxious in a new situation, especially if it is emotionally laden. However, it is the pastor's responsibility to create a milieu in which the parishioner can let down his or her guard and take full advantage of the opportunity to bare his or her soul. We will talk more about how to make the office a safe place later; however, let us talk for a moment about establishing rapport.

Arranging the Office

If a pastor is going to do counseling in his or her office, the office needs to be conducive to the counseling process. Since I do marriage and family therapy in my office, the first thing I had to consider was the size of the office. It is difficult to do pastoral counseling in a very small office. Parishioners who come into the office may already feel trapped, and to come into an office where they have no room to scoot around or stretch out may make them feel even more trapped than before they came.

My desk sits on the side so that I can come out from behind my desk and sit with the person with whom I am counseling. I have a small couch and several chairs where people may sit when they come in. When I invite them into the office I ask them to have a seat and they have the opportunity to sit wherever they choose. I am comfortable operating from any seat in my office, so it doesn't matter to me where they choose to sit. Allowing people this much flexibility is very important when they come into the counseling office for the first time. After the parishioner chooses a seat, I choose my seat close enough so that we can speak in soft tones, but far enough away so that they do not feel encroached upon.

I always make sure that my drapes are open during the daytime so that the natural light of day can come in. On a dark day there may not be enough light to see clearly, but having a view to the outside sends a subliminal message to the counselee that there is a way out. The pastor's office should be situated in a place that allows the parishioner to enter with little or no public view. Many parishioners who go into the pastor's office for counseling would rather that everybody else not know that he or she is going. There may be times when a pastor will choose to do counseling in a different office than where he or she does everything else. It is very helpful to have a bathroom that the parishioners may use, especially to wipe tears from their face before they return to the public. Remember, the parishioners should be comfortable enough in the pastor's office that they may allow themselves to cry freely if need be. But they may not be comfortable when they leave the office and have other people notice that they have been crying.

Last, if a parishioner becomes too comfortable in his or her relationship with the pastor, it may be difficult to refer them to a professional for further work if it becomes necessary. It behooves the pastor to recognize when a referral is needed as soon as possible to avoid going too deep into the dynamics with the parishioner before the referral is made. Much more will be said about this later on.

This chapter will look at three general types of counseling pastors do: premarital, marriage, and issues of faith.

PREMARITAL COUNSELING

When I worked as a chaplain in the hospital, I had a good doctor friend with whom I played Ping-Pong. We established some lifetime relationships on the Ping-Pong table. He was reared with a Ping-Pong table in his basement and had high respect for anyone who could beat him in the game. I could. One day when I was on call overnight and my doctor friend was on call at the same time, I asked him for a Tylenol 3. His response was "Sure, come over here and sit down." He began to examine me and ask me why I wanted this Tylenol pill that was a little stronger than what I could buy across the counter. I challenged him about his formality and said, "I just have a headache and I need a pill." He explained that he was a physician who could not just give out medication without knowing what he was doing. He really hit home when he said to me, "I like you very much, and I would not like to do anything to hurt you."

I thought about this statement he made to me many times after that. How many times did I simply respond to a person's request without really checking out what he or she needed? Was I really as professional in my ministry as my friend was in medicine? How do I know that I won't hurt someone who I really care about if I do not take the time to check him or her out? As a result, I made some rules for myself as a professional minister. Among those rules was that I would not perform a marriage ceremony without doing premarital counseling. I was pleased that I had made that rule when my doctor friend asked me to perform his wedding and I was able to say to him that I had to do premarital counseling with him before I was able to do it. He understood perfectly.

Some pastors go through great lengths and use a lot of psychological tests to determine whether people are suited for each other. My own experience is that when persons have gone to the point of setting a date to get married, nothing I can demonstrate to them with tests, observation, or any other kind of assessment will change their minds about what they intend to do. They may change their minds for some other reason, but not because of anything I can do. Thankfully, because of the premarital counseling I have done, there have been at least two couples who have decided not to get married. There was a third couple who decided initially not to get married, but then decided again to do it, without my knowledge. Their marriage was followed by a painful divorce.

Since the decision whether to get married is literally beyond the scope of the counseling, I focus on those issues that I feel will be most helpful for them, assuming that the marriage is going to take place. The three things that I focus on are money, spirituality, and sexuality. The umbrella under which all of these issues come is communication. The only way to know where each marriage partner is coming from and to resolve any differences that occur between him and her is for them to learn how to effectively communicate.

Money

Of all the dynamics that go on between people who are married, the one that seems to lead them to the divorce court most frequently is money. In fact, the most difficult issue to resolve between married couples (aside from perhaps the children) is money. So, after establishing rapport with the couple, I usually will ask them what they think is the number one reason for divorce. Young couples often do not know. More mature people, especially those who have been married before, immediately answer, "Money." So I ask them, "How will you two handle the money in your marriage?" I often get two or three versions of how the money will be handled. One of them will say, "Oh, I'm going to take care of all of that." The other will say, "Oh, I thought that I was the one who was going to do that." A man once said, "I'll just give it to her and she'll handle that," and the woman retorted back, "I never agreed to that!" My point is made when couples discover how important talking about money is. That led us to a discussion about how to handle money in their relationship.

There is no single way to handle the money in a marriage. No two marriage-finances are the same. Ultimately, I try to lead them into a solution that includes several factors: mutual ownership, mutual access, mutual control, shared chores, and goal setting.

Mutual Ownership

What I mean by mutual ownership is that once a couple is married, it is no longer *his* money or *her* money, but now *their* money. One of the biggest problems I have found in doing marital counseling is that while the couple may be married legally and often emotionally, they never married financially. In many cases they have no idea how much money each of them brings into the relationship. Even worse, they have no idea of what happens to the money, even after it is brought into the relationship. Marriage means oneness, and that means one financially as much as any other way. Until the money brought in by the two persons has become married, they are flirting with disaster in their relationship. The only money that is married in a relationship is the money that is in the same account where both persons have equal ownership.

Mutual Access

I do not encourage married couples to put all of their earnings into one single account. As a matter of fact, it is their decision as to how they handle their money, as I have said before. However, I am a strong advocate of suggesting that a portion of their money go into a joint account. This joint account will usually be the one that pays all the expenses for the house, the food, the insurance, vacations, entertainment, and most of the things that they share commonly. How they divide up those things that they own independently, like clothes, cars, hair appointments, makeup, and so forth, is something they can decide between them. The personal accounts, of course, will be smaller than the large account that covers the major items.

Some people choose not to put the money into a joint account, but to simply divide the common expenses between them. My contention is that unless there is a common pot for at least a portion of their income to be placed, there is no point at which the finances of the couple are really married. It is important that this common pot (regardless of how little or how much money is in it) become a symbol of their marriage. The only way it can serve as that symbol is if they both have mutual access to it. What I mean by "mutual" is that they both have direct access and do not have to access it through the other partner. If they put it under the pillow, they both know which pillow it is under. If they put it in a bank, they both can go to the bank and draw it out or write a check. If they keep it in a jar, either of them can go to the jar and get it when they need it. They both put into it, most likely in different amounts, and they both have total access to it if they need to take it out.

Mutual Control

I usually say to couples about to be married that since money is so closely associated with power in any relationship, they both should have an equal say about how the money is spent. I also say to them that even though they become one in a marriage, a marriage is really three entities: me, thee, and we—mine, yours, and ours. What this means, when it comes to finances, is that there should always be some "me" money that only "me" can control. There should always be some "thee" money that only the other spouse has total control over. However, the "we" money in the marriage should be controlled mutually by both parties.

Regardless of how much each one puts into the pot, once it is in the pot it loses its identity and is no longer attached to its source. It becomes married money and should be controlled equally by both parties in the marriage.

Shared Chores

Taking the responsibility for paying all of the monthly bills is a great chore. It is time-consuming, it can be frustrating, and it requires a level of competence to get it all right. Often in the marriage one person can handle this chore better than the other, and one or the other often will willingly do the chore because it gives them a sense of security. I encourage couples to share this chore at least periodically, the purpose of which is so that they can appreciate what the one who does it all the time is contributing to the marriage. The other reason is, of course, if something happens to the one who does it all the time, the other spouse will be able to pick it up without a lot of orientation.

I once had a couple with which I counseled where the man believed that he should be in charge of all of the money. To him, this meant that it was his responsibility to pay all of the bills. For some very good historical reasons, which I will not go into, he was very poor at this chore and led the family into serious debt. His wife, on the other hand, was very astute at this process and was quite willing to take it on as her responsibility in the marriage. After a long time, I got him to agree to let his wife do it on a trial basis. She did so well that he could not find any reason why she should not continue to do it. Over a period of about two years she had them totally out of debt. He actually earned more money than she did, but she was much more valuable financially to the relationship. I constantly reminded him that he should appreciate her for taking on this tremendous chore.

Goal Setting

A marriage is a living entity. Like all living entities, if it does not grow, it will die. Some couples that have been careful in spending their money find that over a period of time they have amassed a large amount of money that is just sitting around as if waiting for the worst to happen. Trust me when I tell you that there is nothing worse than having a large sum of money sitting around with no particular plan as to what to do with it. While it may have been amassed with the concept of preparing for a rainy day, unless something is done about designating this money, it may cause the rainy day. Even worse is not saving any money because you have no plan for using it; so just let it get away day after day, week after week.

Ask couples the question "Where do you see yourself three to five years from now?" The answer is often having so many children, having a big house, taking trips around the world, and so on. All of these are wonderful dreams to have, and some of them will be realized whether they are planned or not. But it is very helpful for couples to sit down and dream together. One of the things that keeps couples together and helps them to avoid being distracted by other things are the common goals that they have agreed upon and both invest in together. Common goals such as education, career choices, vacations, or early retirement are some of the kinds of goals that couples have agreed upon and which they work toward on a weekly or monthly basis.

We do not have space in this book to talk about the steps that are necessary to realize any of these goals, but suffice it to say that once the goal is agreed upon, there are incremental financial steps that must be taken toward reaching the goal. These steps would hardly allow money to be lying around unassigned to anything at all. The sooner a couple can begin to set common goals and begin working toward them, the sooner their marriage has a common path to travel. Before the goal can become a legitimate marital goal, it must be fully agreed upon by both parties.

Spirituality

After I help the couple to communicate with each other around the issue of finance, we move into the area of spirituality. Spirituality, for me, is more than belief in God, going to church, being a Christian (or some other faith), reading the Bible and praying; spirituality is much broader than religious behavior and belief. It includes values by which we live, attitudes about certain things that are meaningful to each individual, morals, character, and ethical behavior. Spirituality is closely related to philosophy; it includes such issues as what does it mean to be a man, what does it mean to be a woman, what does it mean to be married? It addresses certain issues about boundaries between friends and family members, parenting children, fairness, justice, politics, and worldviews. Each person comes to the marriage from a different spiritual vantage point.

Often there has been little previous discussion about where people are coming from on these various issues and many others. Now, as they are planning to get married, they realize that one partner is extremely conservative and the other is extremely liberal. Or one is a sexist and the other is a feminist. One was reared in a close-knit family and the other was reared pretty much a loner. One believes children should be seen and not heard and the other believes that children come first before everything in the family. It is pointless for them to have these differences revealed to them when they have already set the date to get married. In all likelihood, they will do it anyway. Since I believe that different cultures can get along with each other and really enjoy living together, I make no effort to dissuade persons who are extremely different from coming together as one. I simply try to help them learn some methodology by which they can make this coming together more palatable.

What I try to help couples understand during premarital counseling is regardless of where they have come from, their task is to make a new trail together. When I discuss this issue with the couple, I will draw an upside-down V. At the beginning of one line, I put a symbol for the woman. At the beginning of the other line, I put a symbol for the man and then a symbol where the two lines come together at the top of the upside-down V to indicate where they are now. I say to them, "This is where you have come from individually," pointing to the two wider points at the bottom;

then I say, "This is where you are now" and point to the top of the V where they come together.

We discuss what it has been like for each of them from the beginning of their family life to where they are now. I make the point that they cannot go back and erase or change any of what has happened to them that has made them who they are. Then I draw a long stem from the point that the two lines come together straight up. The upside-down V now becomes an upside-down Y. I say to them that the point where they have come from up to the point where they come together is the road they have traveled individually, and the road above is the road they will travel together. I say to them that it is important that the road they travel together become more prominent than the road they travel individually. The longer and more prominent the road they travel together, the more they become one in their marriage. I also say to them that they may not have had much choice in the experiences they had until now, but they can choose now what they will experience together.

The Oneness Road

I sometimes call this road they travel together the "oneness road." I encourage them not to travel either of the roads that they have taken before but rather to choose together their own road. For example, rather than for him to become a member of her church or her to become a member of his church, they find a church where they both feel comfortable. If they both come to this relationship owning homes, I suggest to them that they should both consider selling their homes and buying a new home together. If she always went to a certain place at Christmas and he always went to another place at Christmas, I suggest that they choose a place that they can go to for themselves or stay home together. Needless to say, these suggestions are rather strident at face value; however, the point is that they need to make their own path and not feel that they must travel the path that their partner established for himself or herself.

I also encourage them to find some brand new things to do together that they can both appreciate. One is to find recreation that suits them both and to find something that they can both volunteer to do. I've seen couples that are very happy in their volunteer work. They started this early in their marriage, and after they retired they had something to keep them busy for the rest of their lives. Sometimes it is at the church, at the school, in the community, at the political polls, and so on. The important thing is, it is something they can create and share a path they can walk together. By blazing their own path, they develop a new spirituality that is theirs together, and they are not limited to the spirituality they brought into the relationship.

Sexuality

Some people think sexuality is copulating, or at least those behaviors that lead to copulation. This could not be further from the truth. Sexuality is as much a part of who a person is as is personality. Sexuality is always going on throughout the day and does not wait until night to become a part of a couple's reality. It has to do with identity, self-esteem, self-image, sense of adequacy, quality of intimacy, sense of security, and need to control. Sexuality begins in the morning when people brush their teeth, go through the grooming process, decide what to wear for the day, and say good-bye. In spite of the fact that young married couples may have a lot of energy to invest in sexual intercourse, most of sexuality has little to do, if anything, with sexual intercourse. Sexuality has to do with how one is seen by one's peers, how one relates with the opposite sex, how one is seen in one's own family, and how one works every day.

When I talk about sexuality in premarital counseling, I usually focus on three things: (1) boundaries, (2) preservation of dignity, and (3) individual growth.

Boundaries

If a couple is going to remain together as a couple, they must accept that their marriage is their primary relationship; and as such their relationship has boundaries and priorities. Being one means that nothing comes between them at all—not the past, not the future, not parents, not family, not friends, not even children. Many couples get into difficulty when they bring children into a marriage, because new boundaries have to be negotiated. Trouble especially occurs when one of the couple puts the children before the spouse. While I have seen this in women more often, it happens with men as well. This does not mean that children should be abandoned; on the contrary, the spouse needs to negotiate with his or her spouse to take care of the children and even elicit the spouse's help to do so. This is more desirable than to polarize the situation and make it an either/or situation.

Indicators of the marriage being the primary relationship include where the couple spend their time and money, what they talk about most, and what they teach their children about the marriage relationship. Children have a difficult time when a parent remarries, and it is understandable that parents would like to make life easier for them. But a parent cannot protect children from reality, and one should not try, especially at the expense of a marriage. Needless to say, it is inappropriate to go to the opposite extreme, where one neglects the children in favor of the marriage partner.

Another place where couples have boundary difficulties is with in-laws. Many individuals have never differentiated themselves from their family of origin. Their concept of marriage is to bring another person into the family, rather than putting some space between themselves and their family. This is particularly true when the parents of the family of origin are overly involved in the relationship of the new couple. It is interesting how many mothers will not let their sons go, especially when he chooses to marry. To compound the problem, a man who has never emotionally left home, yet sees himself as head of the marriage household, is really having his house ruled by his mother. So there is a tug-of-war over this man between his mother and his wife. A solution to this boundary problem is quite similar to the upside-down Y. A couple must learn to make their own decisions and refuse to give in to powerful influences outside of the marriage.

This is true whether they are her friends, his drinking buddies, her parents, his parents, or whoever it may be. Part of being committed to a marriage is being committed to detaching oneself from outside influences. When I see this as a problem in premarital counseling, I realize that I will be seeing this couple again in marital counseling.

Preservation of Dignity

There are things that will be shared in a marriage that *will not be* and *should never be* shared with anybody else. One of the blessings of marriage is the quality of intimacy. That intimacy can only be achieved with the assurance of privacy and confidentiality. Nobody wants the world to know what they have said behind closed doors and how they have behaved when they let down their guard. I'm shocked by some of the things that are shown on TV and how easily married couples are seduced into violating the dignity of their partners on national television. It is more or less an unwritten rule that there are certain things that happen between a man and a woman that should never be shared with a third party.

One of the reasons most states have moved to incompatibility as the only reason necessary for divorce, instead of the way it used to be where you had to prove certain things about your spouse, is because persons' dignity was violated simply for the purpose of getting divorced, destroying some but hurting all. Sharing what has happened between a married couple with other people is a violation of privacy. Some people have gotten into serious legal trouble for setting up secret cameras to spy on a spouse. Regardless of how much a couple may become angry with each other or how big a fight they may have between them, the one thing they should be careful not to do is to violate each other's dignity. Once that has happened, it is very difficult, if at all possible, to ever reach that level of intimacy and trust again.

Individual Growth

One of the reasons for divorce is that one of the partners outgrows the other. Growth is natural in all individuals as they continue to have experiences from year to year. It is the one who does not grow but who remains the same that is unnatural in a marriage. Not only should marriage partners find ways to continue to grow, but they also need to support each other in their individual growth. Couples should use not only words of encouragement but also the family finances when necessary. Sometimes it is necessary to reallocate responsibilities in the family for a period of time to allow one to grow—for example taking a college course.

At one time in our history, some women found it difficult to grow because they spent all of their time with only children and chores. It is important that women (and men) find ways to grow by working outside of the home in some capacity, either by volunteer work or paid work. Some can even benefit by using the Internet in the home. The point is that each person learns what is going on in society—in the outside world. If a woman happens to be a stay-at-home mother, it is to her advantage to keep her mind occupied with issues that are meaningful to her and her family. If she allows her husband to grow too far beyond her, it becomes a problem in their marriage.

Men who fail to grow do not do so mostly because they are so tied down at home, but rather because they are tied down to their old ways. One of the first things that a married man needs to do is to find another community of friends with which to do things. Hanging out in the old places and doing the same old things do not help a man to grow. Growth is not necessarily something that happens naturally or easily; one must set goals and work toward them. While it is a good thing for a man to grow in any case, it is especially necessary if he has a wife who is committed to her own growth.

These are pivotal issues to focus on in premarital counseling, and they all require intentional communication between the prospective spouses. Unless the couple learns how to communicate effectively, they will not be able to move forward on these issues. If you suspect a communication problem, spend extra time to specifically focus on communication skills.

MARITAL COUNSELING

Marital counseling can take an inordinate amount of time, effort, and energy. Therefore, it is not always a good idea for a pastor to do marriage counseling with parishioners. In addition, it changes the relationship between the pastor and the couple, it may be very embarrassing to the couple, and the dynamics may be much deeper than the pastor is prepared to handle. Yet every marriage has some scrapes and fights from time to time. Sometimes people just need someone that they both respect to listen to their particular story and help them reconcile. Sometimes one or both members of the marriage simply need a space where they can share their feelings and say they are sorry. If these dynamics continue to show up in a marriage, however, it can be an indication that this marriage needs some serious work. The sooner the pastor makes a referral to a marriage and family therapist or a pastoral counselor, the better.

Even with the help a pastor gives a couple in resolving their differences, it should be the couple that determines what the solution to the problem is. Once a pastor gets into the business of recommending solutions, it does one of two things: it makes the couple dependent on the pastor to resolve their conflicts, and it makes the pastor responsible for whether the solution works or not. Resolution of conflict is a healthy thing; and if the pastor can facilitate this without getting too involved, it is a good intervention. I strongly recommend to pastors that they limit their marital counseling to three to five sessions at the most. If the issue is something deeper than this, you need to make an immediate referral.

ISSUES OF FAITH

Our lives are so complex and filled with so much information from so many different vantage points that people are really confused about their faith. Whenever someone comes to my office to talk about an issue of faith, I am both gratified and apprehensive. Gratified because I am pleased that a person is really seeking to make the right decision, and apprehensive because I feel inadequate to the task of helping people find the truth they seek. It would be so much easier if a pastor could simply quote a biblical text and assume that everything would fall neatly into place. But matters of the heart and soul are so complex these days that it is difficult to find an appropriate text, let alone the interpretation that is acceptable to solve the dilemma.

There are some things that a pastor should keep in mind when helping people with issues of faith:

(1) It is not a real issue unless it is attached to an event in life. What I mean by this is that people will sometimes come to the office asking general questions and essentially wanting a theological explanation for something very general. Much like the teenager who comes to a counselor and says, "I have a friend with a problem." Whatever answers you give to people who have not owned up to what really motivated them to ask the question will most likely be the wrong answer. If they come to the office raising an issue of faith, the pastor needs to know what motivated them to come. Be sure that you get to the bottom of the issue they are raising before you try to respond.

I ran into a woman I had not talked to in about two years. She was doing fine and was eager to tell me how she had done exactly what I told her to do and how it had changed her life. The last time we talked, she was living with a man who was attending law school. This had been going on for some time, and she was the only one working and taking care of the home and him. She was angry, frustrated, and felt betrayed because he had promised to get a job after finishing another degree he was working on before but instead went to law school. After venting all of her feelings to me, she asked what I thought she should do. I was very careful, as I always am, in discussing matters of the heart and soul; I wanted to be sure that no matter what happened, it would not be due to my advice. So I asked her what she wanted to do.

She said she was going to give him until June, since he would graduate in April, to get a job. After that, if he did not get a job, she would put him out. She needed to know if this was fair and would God expect anything more of her? She was really proud of herself for coming to this decision. I responded, "Sounds like you really mean it this time." She said, "I sure do." I smiled and gave her a hug, which she said she really needed. Now, two years later, she has put him out and found another man she really loves and who loves her, and it is all because of me. I protested that I never told her to put him out. She emphatically quoted me as saying in no uncertain terms, "If he doesn't get a job by June, put him out." She was so thankful for my help. Look from where she had come; she will probably be sending me a wedding invitation soon. She gave me a big hug and said, "You are wonderful!" With that, she was off and gone.

I then further rehearsed for weeks the conversation that I had had with her two years before. She had approached me about the issue of whether a man and a woman should live together without the benefit of marriage. She had been living with a man for about three years then. I knew better than to get caught in that old trap of giving definite advice after hearing only one side of the story, or giving direct advice in any case. I remember she had wanted me to quote to her a scripture that supported her putting him out because he refused to get a job. I am sure to that request I most likely quoted Paul: "If anyone will not work, neither shall he eat" (2 Thess. 3:10 NKJV). With this statement, the damage was done. People often come to the pastor with the express purpose of having the pastor agree with what they have already decided to do. A pastor needs to be sure to get the full story, even before falling into that warm, soothing pool of quoting scriptures. Had I run into this woman before she was happily in love with a new man, I may have really been in trouble with her.

(2) Two different issues can raise essentially the same faith question, but the answer for each will be different. The pastor needs to know that there is never one single answer for any particular issue. Sometimes the parishioner will push the pastor for *the truth*, but truth is somewhat like medicine: it is all good, but it must be administered in the proper dosage to different people. What is truth for one may not be truth for another.

(3) Similar to number 2, the ultimate answer to any issue of faith must come from the individual raising the question. No matter what information you give to a person or persons, until they are ready to receive and embrace it, it is of no value to them. People are much more ready to accept what they come up with themselves. They will tell you they accept what you tell them in the office, but as soon as they are out of the office, the fears and confusion that brought them in at first will take over again, and they cannot act on what you have shared with them. However, if the information comes from within them, they own it; it is part of them and they can use it.

With these understandings about issues of faith, the pastor needs to know the story and event behind the question. What has motivated the person to come raising this issue at this particular time? What is the real issue they are raising? Sometimes people are not sure what the issue is, and you need to help them first focus on the issue itself. Once the issue is clear, the pastor needs to question what the individual feels in his or her own heart about this issue. Help them understand what their own truth is about the issue. Often persons have already come up with the proper answer to the dilemma, but they need only for the pastor to affirm where they are. The pastor's task is then only to reflect back to them what they are saying to the pastor. The pastor is like a mirror that reflects their truth back into their face. Persons can usually do their own "faith grooming" if they can see what they are saying and what the problems are.

Finally, the pastor's job is to affirm that they have arrived at the solution they were seeking. They have found the place to resolve the issue they were raising without violating their sense of faith. If the pastor feels that they are violating their faith, he or she may raise the question. Again, the individual must make the adjustment and then the pastor affirms the adjustment the person has made.

Of course there are times when the parishioner cannot come up with a realistic solution, at least not one that the pastor can affirm. Part of the counseling process is for the pastor to help the parishioner generate realistic options. Sometimes the issue is too complicated to find a reasonable solution in a short time. The pastor must remember that counseling is a process; immediate solutions don't always exist in these matters. Often when there is no clear direction to take, there may be a need for more information. The pastor needs to point out what information is needed to make a better assessment. This is where most pastors and parishioners make their biggest mistakes—trying to find a solution without all of the pertinent data. One small piece of information can change the entire picture.

Another issue is that of affirming the decision that the parishioner makes. The pastor should always affirm parishioners' right and responsibility to make their own decisions; after all, they are the ones who have to live with them. To insist or encourage parishioners to accept the pastor's remedy will at best foster dependency, and at worst make the pastor responsible for the parishioner trying something that does not work. Affirming the parishioner to make his or her own decision is not the same as affirming the decision that the parishioner makes. It is not uncommon that the pastor will have to say, "I would not do that if it were me; but if you are sure that is what you want to do, it is your decision."

Frequently this kind of situation comes up in premarital counseling. I can recall many cases where parishioners came to me believing that they had found the perfect one for them to marry. In one case, a young woman came to me to talk about marrying a man. She had not known him very long, and what she did know about him raised questions for her about his integrity. The more we talked, the more I realized that marrying this man would be a mistake. Her heart was set on marriage, but I was strongly against it, and she listened to me and decided not to marry him. This happened early in my career; I did not realize that unless the parishioner makes the decision, he or she may not ultimately accept it. Three months later, the parishioner changed her mind and married the man anyway. One of the issues for her was that he was Roman Catholic and she was Baptist. He persuaded her to have a priest marry them. Four months later the marriage was over, the woman had all of her clothes and furniture destroyed, and she was afraid for her life. The pastor cannot live the parish-ioner's life from his or her office; it is the right and responsibility of the parishioner to live his or her own life. The pastor must affirm that right but not the decision that the parishioner makes.

THE PASTOR'S ROLE AND AUTHORITY

Counseling, by virtue of its nature, gives the pastor more authority. The authority comes in the contract that is agreed upon by the pastor and the one or ones that he or she is counsel-ing. The term *contract* sounds rather formal, especially if the min-ister is seeing one of his or her own parishioners. What is necessary is that the pastor and parishioner have an understand-ing and agreement of what is expected of the pastor and the process. This *agreement* gives the pastor the authority to chal-lenge, confront, analyze, assess, and give direction. I give my clients homework in between the sessions. Sometimes they have legitimate reasons for not doing it, and sometimes I tell them to go back and do it and not make another appointment until it's done. I have had clients who have had problems with intimacy that manifested itself in their lovemaking. On occasion, when it was appropriate and the circumstances allowed it, I have told couples they could not make love again until I told them to. I have required that couples or perhaps one member of the couple get a full physical examination before they return for counseling.

I try to do a complete history on persons I counsel. When a pastor is trying to help a parishioner sort through some options related to an issue, it may be necessary for the pastor to have some background information. Without knowing something about the parishioner's history, the pastor is shooting in the dark trying to help. Some of the questions I ask them are extremely embarrassing, and some are very painful and frightening. I push for the answer to these questions at some point in the process because they are necessary to be able to assess what is going on with the client. Even though I consider myself a client-centered therapist, meaning that I try to follow the client's agenda, it is the client who is in charge. I still am very much aware that I have a lot of authority in the counseling sessions and could set the agenda, but generally I let the parishioner set the agenda for our time together.

The other thing about counseling is that a fee *is usually paid when counseling is continued for an extended period of time*. Whether a pastor should collect a fee from his or her own parishioners is a very controversial issue. Persons will only work as hard as they feel the work is valuable. If it doesn't cost them anything, they have no way to measure its value. Even when I counseled with teenagers, I would require them to pay some of their own fees so that they would have some sense of the value they were getting. If they had no money, I made them do some work in exchange for the counseling.

Some pastors believe that counseling is a part of their responsibility as pastors. This is true if their counseling is limited to short-term situations that are little more than pastoral care. However, if a pastor is trained to do long-term marriage and family therapy, he or she may be wise to charge a fee. The fee is set by the counselor/pastor. Again, this demonstrates the authority of the pastor. Oftentimes when I have counseled parishioners in my own church, I have given them a discount on their fee. But if a pastor does not charge any fee at all, he or she may find that he or she is spending most of the time counseling and not having time to do the other things that need to be done.

RITUALS AND ETIQUETTE

Some pastors begin their sessions with a prayer and close with a prayer. If they ask the parishioners, they will find that sometimes the parishioners tolerate this ritual because they feel it is important to the pastor. Some pastors begin each session with a handshake and conclude each session with hugs. Some insurance companies now will not cover a pastor who touches the parishioner in any form at all. Rather than to practice rituals for the sake of ritual, I like to reserve rituals that help to reach the goal that the pastor and parishioner are pursuing together.

For example, I had a counselee who was the eighth of nine children. She felt that she had never gotten any love from her mother, as did the other children. By now she was about thirty years old and sadly grieving that she had never gotten from her mother what she had hoped to get. I am not aware of any ritual where you get from your mother what you have never gotten. So we made one up. I suggested that she call her mother and get from her a stole or a quilt or something that had been close to her mother's body. She retrieved one of her mother's favorite blankets that she had had on the bed for a long time. I had her take this blanket, wrap it around her in the chair in the counseling office, and think of it as her mother holding her in her lap.

As she put the blanket around her and sat in the chair, in a short time she began to smile. She could feel her mother embracing her. I told her to take the blanket home and use it as much as necessary until she felt that she had all that she could get from her mother. Years later when I ran into her she informed me that she was still using the blanket. This had become a ritual for her that changed her attitude toward her mother and her siblings. She felt better about them and herself. If it worked for *Peanuts'* Linus, why not for her?

I have had counselees write letters to people who were dead, write poetry, stand in the mirror and say things to themselves that gave them a more positive self-image, eat some ice cream to celebrate an achievement, and so on. These kinds of rituals seem to help people achieve the goals that they are pursuing. I got the idea years ago from a beer commercial on television that said, "Celebrate all of those victories!" If a person can use a beer to celebrate a victory, you can celebrate with anything healthy that gives you a positive feeling of achievement.

I am a hugger, and I still hug people in the counseling session; however, I usually hug them to celebrate having done a good job of achieving a goal that they were striving toward. They already know I care about them, but the hug adds a little something extra for the hard work they do. Making changes in a person's life is a very difficult thing to do, and there should always be a ritual to celebrate the rite of passage for making a tremendous change.

DILEMMAS

Confidentiality

In this section I want to talk about two things: *referral* and *confidentiality*. Let's talk about confidentiality first. More than in any other ministry that a pastor may do, when he or she is counseling with a couple or an individual, what happens in the session must be held in *strictest confidence*. The reason that the counseling process works in part is because the individuals know that they can say anything in any way at any time, and it will never be repeated again to anybody. This means you cannot go home and talk about it with your spouse, you can't talk about it with your colleagues, and you can't use the dynamics as sermon illustrations a month later. It is so secret that you hardly remember it ever happened. Not only is this expected of a professional, but it is also necessary for the process to work.

Trust is one of the main characteristics that sets the pastor apart from many other persons with whom the parishioner may engage. All of that trust could go down the drain if the pastor ever revealed anything that was said. It is a good thing to keep some notes on situations; however, I keep notes as sparingly as possible so that they can prompt me to remember but not necessarily give information to anybody else. Wherever the files on counselees are kept, they must be locked at all times.

As soon as I say that you must keep everything in strictest confidence, I must also say that a pastor should not do counseling in isolation. There should always be colleagues or a person the counselor can go to to make sure that he or she is keeping things in perspective. With that person or persons one must share at least the dynamics of the case he or she is working on to get appropriate feedback. This is to the counselee's advantage, and most counselees will appreciate knowing that their pastor is getting help in helping them. Any pastor who has no place to talk about issues that come up in his or her counseling is running a serious risk for liability. At the very least, a counselor needs to have a peer with whom he or she is able to share what he or she is doing in counseling to get some objective feedback.

Confidentiality has its limits, at least in some states. There are laws in some states that consider conversations between pastors and parishioners to be the same as confession (like between priests and Catholic parishioners, or lawyers and clients). In these states the pastor has little to worry about in most cases; however, one can never be sure of anything where legal matters are concerned, especially in this litigious society. In the states where pastoral conversation is not protected by law, a pastor may be called as a witness in marriage and family issues. All the notes that are kept are subject to subpoena. In most states, if the pastor becomes aware of anything that is life threatening to the counselee or someone else, it must be reported. Such things as child or adult abuse, threat of suicide, or homicide *must* be reported. Perhaps I should say that confidentiality must be maintained to the limit of the pastor's power.

Referral

As I mentioned in brief detail earlier, pastors should always have a referral network available to them. The pastor should have a psychiatrist, psychologist, marriage and family therapist, pastoral counselor, lawyer, social worker, various doctors, nurses, and so on, that he or she can refer people to. This network should not be numbers that they have gotten out of the telephone book, but persons that they either know personally or through someone that they do know personally. *Never refer someone blindly.* That means do not refer someone to someone you do not know and where you cannot say what the outcome of relating with that person will be. Whenever I hear speakers or become aware of people who I believe would be a good person to refer to, I make it my business to get to know as much about them as possible and to write their names and numbers in my book for future use.

There are also signs that suggest referral that pastors need to know. It is not fair for the parishioner to go to the pastor's office, break down and cry and tell their story for several sessions, then wind up being referred and have to go through all of that again. For the parishioner's benefit, if a referral is to be made, it should happen as quickly as possible. A parishioner that has become attached to the pastor and his or her style of counseling may be more difficult to refer. The sooner the pastor can identify that a referral needs to be made and make the referral, the better it is for all concerned.

Referring a client does not let the pastor off the hook. The pastor is still the parishioner's pastor and should maintain a pastoral relationship with the parishioner even though that parishioner is going for other professional help. As the referral agent, the pastor has the right to call the person to whom the referral was made for the parishioner, and vice versa, to talk about what is best for the parishioner. This is known as professional courtesy. It's not necessary or even advisable for the pastor to know what is going on in the session, but only to know if things are going well and if there is some way he or she may be able to help.

Sometimes all the pastor needs to do is to affirm the person and encourage him or her to continue to go to the sessions. It is helpful to understand that counseling is challenging and that counselees sometimes get to a certain point and must quit for a while until they are ready and/or able to go back and face up to some issues that are difficult for them. Remember, if the counseling is working, it means the parishioner is making some drastic changes. Change is not easy and can only come so much at a time. As clients learn more about themselves, they may feel differently about themselves and that they are now unacceptable to the pastor. It is helpful for them to know that the pastor still accepts them, affirms them, and cares about them. Knowing this, parishioners will often return and continue the counseling process that is necessary for their health.

We all have limitations; why should pastors be any different? And why feel like a failure for recognizing them? Counseling is a serious, long-term business; and the sooner a pastor realizes that he or she has reached his or her limitations and needs to make a referral, the better it is for all concerned.

RESOURCES

It is helpful for a minister to understand the dynamics of counseling and be able to theologize about circumstances that people experience in life. As a theologian, a pastor should be able to talk about people's issues and problems in theological language. Persons' emotional and physical distress always has theological implications. Some people cannot accept what happens in the psychologist's or another therapist's office unless the pastor can put it in a theological framework. Once the pastor can talk about it theologically, it makes sense to parishioners and they are able to accept it and make the necessary changes.

For example, a woman was struggling with her anger toward her mother. Her therapist had said to her that she needed to forgive and move on. She went to see her pastor to explain why she could not just forgive her mother, who continued to interfere with her life. The pastor said, "The Scriptures say that we should honor our parents." With this reminder of the theological injunction, she was much more willing to work on getting along with her mother. Many people have not internalized religious values, and they need to be reminded from time to time what is expected of them.

A pastor's office should be a place of safety and serenity. The pastor needs to make sure that his or her office is in a safe place and is safely laid out. In the pastor's office that pastor has much authority and should use it effectively, but with restraint. People come to the pastor's office because they need help; a good pastor will enable them to help themselves.

SEVEN

IN THE JAIL

I f you have read a statistic about jails recently, it probably said that they were overcrowded. Courts are requiring some jails to release inmates early because there is not enough room for them. Many jails are at double the capacity that they were built to retain. A recent statistic indicated that nearly 50 percent of African American young men between the ages of sixteen and twenty-four are in some way connected to the correctional system. This means that they are either in jail, in prison, on bond, on probation, or something related.

There was a time when only a few women would be found in jails, but today women are going to jail in greater numbers. With the continuation of high unemployment, drug enforcement programs, and the zero-tolerance policies that some administrations stress, many more female members of our society are seeing the inside of jails. In the wake of the September 11, 2001, terrorist attacks, law enforcement at every level is much more intense and serious about its business. What does this mean to the average pastor? It means that in all likelihood a part of your ministry will be visiting parishioners in jail. It may even mean that you will specialize in jail ministry.

Depending on the culture of your congregation, one in four of your young men may have been involved in the correctional system at any given time. Not only the young, but, because of the many tragedies that have taken place as a result of domestic violence, young and old, women and men, and girls and boys are being arrested and taken to jail even for their first involvement. If you don't think it is going to affect you as a pastor, you are not paying attention.

ESTABLISHING RAPPORT

Jail is the one place you do not want to go to unless you do have good relationships with staff. The sound of the heavy steel door closing and locking behind when you go into jail is enough in itself to scare many people straight. The rules about entering in and visiting with people are endless. In many cases they seem, and are, inhumane; but they are necessary, or at least somebody thinks they are. Regardless of how distasteful the rules may be, they are enforced to the letter of the law. When a pastor goes into the jail, this is one place where he or she has absolutely no power, at least not going in; but relationship with the staff can change a lot of that.

Jail

There is a difference between jail and prison. The jail is the holding place, for the most part, for people who have been accused of a crime but not yet convicted and sentenced (there are a few people in jail serving short sentences). The only reason they are there is because their crime was so serious that the court was afraid to let them go, or because they do not have enough money to pay the bond required to release them. Many of them are highly agitated, angry, anxious, scared, and embarrassed. Their future is uncertain and the waiting is atrocious. They have very little communication with their lawyers most of the time; and so many of them send letters to the judge that even if the judge were eager to answer, it would be difficult—if at all possible—to keep up with the demand.

The common joke in jail is that nobody is guilty of anything: nobody did it, they are making a mistake, it wasn't my fault, I am innocent. If a person admits to a crime, he or she is considered crazy or trying to impress somebody. It is very important that high security is maintained for people in jail. Some of them know that unless they find a way to escape, they may spend the rest of their life behind bars.

Prison

Prison is different; the trial has already taken place and the sentence has been handed down. For most people it is just a matter of settling in and doing their time. They find ways to spend time to pass the days away. Some of them volunteer to work, go to school, study on their own, or continue to try to control their lives and those around them to whatever degree they can. Many of them even turn to religion as a way to live with their present condition and keep from returning to their old situations once they are released from prison. Most inmates who have been in jail and prison will say that prison time is much easier to do than jail time.

ESTABLISHING A PASTORAL RELATIONSHIP WITH STAFF

In an effort to establish rapport with officers it is important to have some appreciation for the kind of personality that a pastor will be relating to. One way to look at officers in the jails is to put them in one of two categories: (1) those who generally view inmates as good people who made a mistake, in other words, a good person who is broken and needs to be fixed; and (2) those who view inmates as persons who broke the law and should be punished. In spite of which group these officers may fall into, the one thing they have in common is that they know they must apply the rules where inmates are concerned. You will seldom find them tolerating nonsense when it comes to doing their work. One lapse of judgment or concentration could be disastrous for them and everybody else.

Many of the officers, including the ones who believe inmates have done wrong and should be punished, will bend over backwards to help inmates get every break and opportunity for rehabilitation that they can. Generally speaking, most officers are in this business to help society, and that means not only the government, especially corrections, and the public at large, but also the inmates themselves.

Most of the jail officers welcome ministers who come to visit inmates. They have had experiences with ministers who try to bend the rules, argue about the rules, and conduct themselves in less than a professional manner; and they have experienced ministers as inmates. In spite of the fact that they recognize that ministers are not perfect, for the most part they are still open to receiving ministers and assisting in providing pastoral care to inmates. As a minister introduces himself or herself to an officer, it is helpful to understand that officers who retain inmates are in some ways as much inmates as the prisoners. When I was a chaplain in a jail, the officers were in steel cages where they controlled everything on that floor. When I related with them, I related with them through the bars, as I did with the inmates. They could not come out of the cage at any time until another officer relieved them. Sometimes, with the exception of the noise they heard from the cells, their time on shift was spent without much communication or stimulation. I found most of them very eager to meet me and talk to me about anything that was worthwhile conversation. I have had the same experience in other jails that I have visited. My students and professional colleagues verify that relating with officers in a jail is not a difficult task if one is honest and straightforward.

Like inmates, officers are constantly sizing up anyone they meet to see how real they are. Not everyone who goes into a jail with ministerial credentials is real about their profession and who they are personally. It is important for the officers to discern the difference, because not knowing could mean a breach of security.

Many jails have chaplains, and those that do not often have someone who serves in that capacity, even though he or she may not have ministerial credentials. Any minister visiting a jail should make contact with the chaplain before he or she goes to the jail and immediately upon entering the jail. The chaplains can open doors for the pastor that could never open otherwise. The visitation policies can be so stringent that it is a debasing experience to try to visit someone with full security in force. Chaplains can relax some of this security and allow private, hands-on kinds of visitation for pastors. Once the pastor has achieved a good rapport with the chaplain (or whoever is acting in that role) it is much easier to establish rapport throughout the jail. If no chaplain (or substitute thereof) is available, the ideal person to develop a relationship with is the jail commander. The jail commander is like the warden in a prison; he or she has authority to do whatever is necessary for the pastors to gain the access that they need. Some people in this role are called *superintendents*. Whatever the title, the authority is the same. It is the person who runs the facility and is the one with whom the pastor should have a good relationship.

ESTABLISHING A PASTORAL RELATIONSHIP WITH INMATES

In most cases, unless an inmate is charged with a very serious crime or has committed crimes in the past, that inmate will be released on bond. And it is true that there are inmates in jail who are innocent of the charges against them. This does not mean they are innocent, but innocent of the charges. The pastor's role is not to determine innocence or guilt. The pastor's role is to relate with the inmate and be supportive of the inmate spiritually and emotionally. Just to show up at all at the jail is a tremendous manifestation of pastoral care to the inmate. Not all pastors are able or willing to go through all that they must to visit an inmate in jail.

If a pastor has a history with the inmate, the pastor's voice may have meaning in setting bail. Bail is the amount of money that must be paid for the person to be released pending the trial. If the crime is very serious or there is some reason to believe that the person may not show up for the trial, the judge will set the bail very high. The pastor's interest and influence could help bring the bail amount down.

If the pastor can honestly say that the inmate is one of his or her parishioners who has been active in the church for a number of years, or that the church supports this parishioner in every way and trusts that the parishioner will be available at the time of trial, this may be helpful to the judge in determining what the bail will be. But pastors should be careful to state only what they know firsthand; what family members and friends convey to the pastor may be biased (either for or against) because of their personal relationship.

Once the bail is set, it is often too high for the average person to pay out of his or her pocket. This means that they would have to acquire a *bond*, which is literally an insurance policy to ensure that they will show up for trial. The cost of the bond is usually 10 percent of the total bail. The 10 percent of the bail is the premium that is paid for the bond, and it is not refundable. If the total bail is paid, the bail is returned once the person's trial is disposed of. This is expensive, but since most bails are beyond what a person can pay, they have no choice but to resort to the bond if they want to get out of jail. If you have in your network a bondsman to whom you can refer the parishioner, sometimes it will make it easier for the parishioner to receive a bond.

Bondsmen have rules they must follow related to the collateral for the insurance that they are selling. It is illegal to provide a bond for someone who does not pay the 10 percent. Not all bonding companies are ethical in their business with inmates, and there have been instances where inmates have been released on bond only to resort to burglary and theft to pay the bonds on which they were released.

Sometimes it is a good thing for people to stay in jail for a while. The pastor needs to be willing to face up to this. I have talked to parents who were willing to put up their house, their cars, their jewelry, or anything else of value that they had for a bond collateral. These same parents have spent thousands of dollars getting their son or daughter out of jail on various occasions. Knowing that Mom and Dad will always do whatever it takes to get them out of jail makes it much easier for the son or daughter to ignore the urges to get treatment for whatever is keeping them in trouble. I have said to parents on occasion, "You will be doing your son or daughter a disservice if you bond them out of jail. At some point, they need to learn what it is like to be imprisoned, and your continued effort to save them is simply playing into their pathology."

This is codependent behavior by the parent, who is thus enabling the child to continue his or her destructive behavior by always bailing him or her out. To let a son or daughter stay in jail even overnight creates intolerable guilt for some parents, even if it is for the child's good. Only a pastor can help parents deal with this guilt and do the right thing for their son or daughter.

RELATING WITH POLICE

The police and ministers have one thing in common: they both have a public trust. That is, the public trusts them to do the right thing, to make good decisions, and to foster security for everybody. The police and ministers are natural partners once they get to know each other. One of the things I have done with students as a part of their training, and which I also did as a part of my training, was to ride in a police car with the officers. They accepted me in the car with them and had basically only one question:: "When we get to a situation that we have to get out and take care of, are you going to sit in the car or are you going with us?" Of course I didn't want to miss anything, so I said, "Hey,

I'm with you guys." That was just what they wanted to hear, and as quickly as I responded I was one of them.

But a couple of our calls scared me very badly. For one call we drove at a high rate of speed with only the benefit of a siren to clear the path. The other call was a response to a domestic situation where it was pitch-dark and we had to use flashlights to even see how to get to the house. I admit I was walking next to the officer who was carrying the flashlight, and I put some distance between him and me in case someone shot at the light. I learned to respect these officers and their courage. They also asked my opinion about things and accepted my consultation. I have always related with the police differently since that time and have not had any problem winning their confidence.

Police officers are trained to be tough, and some of them really are; but I have known a number of people who have good relationships with the police because they respect them, and in turn the police respect them. Police officers have a lot of authority, especially on the road. Much is left to their judgment, and a pastor can make a big difference in the ultimate conclusion that they draw. Treat them as partners, not enemies, and they will give you the best they have to offer.

RELATING WITH LAWYERS

Most of the lawyers I know are so sure of themselves that it leads one to believe that there is only one possible conclusion to be drawn from any particular event. That is not true. All that a lawyer can offer is his or her opinion. That opinion may be based on lots of experience, years of education, and an awareness of the dynamics involved; however, it is still an opinion and can always be challenged by another lawyer who will have a different opinion. As long as we are talking about opinions, why not consider a pastoral opinion? If a lawyer intimidates a pastor, that lawyer will likely sense that intimidation and eat the pastor alive. It is important that a pastor really be well-grounded in who he or she is whenever he or she visits a jail, relates with inmates, relates with police, and especially when he or she relates to lawyers. Lawyers are not the enemy; they are simply trained to be adversarial. Pastors are trained to be adversarial as well; they just happen to have a different idea of who the real enemy is.

Don't get hooked into knowing more about the law than the lawyer. Stay in the arena where you are comfortable and powerful; you represent God, Christ, and the church. God is about love, not law; peace, not punishment; commitment, not conviction; and freedom, not imprisonment. Be relational in all your dealings with lawyers; you will find that lawyers are human beings too and that they know how to feel and how to relate.

Pastoral Role and Authority

In jails and prisons with police, lawyers, and inmates, a pastor has no inherent authority. However, through the power of relationship a pastor can influence everything that happens. The people who work with the law and law enforcement must necessarily set aside part of their humanity to be able to do their jobs effectively. They cannot let their emotions carry them away; they cannot be swayed by idealistic theories; they cannot afford to be empathic with the people they are responsible for. Yet they do have families, they do have feelings, and sometimes they need to be reminded of their humanity. The pastor brings to the table the issue of humanity, which nobody else in the system may be thinking about. The pastor brings the concepts of forgiveness, tolerance, grace, and hope. Without the pastor, a person in the system may simply be a statistic, a number, or a case. With the pastor involved, a person has a face and a character. Pastors add new dimensions to the legal process—spirituality and theology.

There are two things pastors must remember if they are going to be effective in legal proceedings: (1) the pastor's ability to relate with persons in these systems makes everything happen— no relationship, no access; and (2) pastors must never think of themselves as higher or better than others performing their particular roles. Even though the pastor may represent God in the situation, pastors must see themselves as part of the team rather than as a higher authority. The pastor needs to think about how everyone can win rather than how to show somebody up. Jails and prisons are already full; judges are looking for alternatives to sending more people to them. If the pastor can offer a reasonable alternative, it may well get serious attention.

RITUALS AND ETIQUETTE

People who are in jail or on bond pending a court action (even if they are released on their own recognizance) are in serious need of all the rituals of the church. If they are in jail, the pastor needs to go to the jail to have prayer, scripture, and communion with them. If they are out of jail but still wards of the court, they need special prayer, scripture, and communion. Since these rituals are sustaining even in good times, they are needed even more when the parishioner is facing the dilemma of court action. Ultimately, all ministers have as their number one responsibility to help save those who are lost. As pastors minister to their parishioners who are in legal trouble, other persons who are in legal trouble will see the pastor's commitment, love, and grace toward this person and may be drawn to Christ as a result. We never know how many people we are benefiting when we love those who are difficult to love.

Confidentiality

Many inmates need to share things that they have held in for a long time. They can only share these things with someone they trust not to judge them and not to betray them. Much of what it means to be a pastor is keeping confidences. The only things that a minister is permitted to break confidence about are issues that have life and death consequences, such as homicide or suicide, child abuse, and in some states abuse of adults. If an inmate says that he or she plans to kill somebody or to kill himself or herself, the pastor is required to report this. Otherwise, pastors are not required to report anything that they hear. There are some prosecutors who would challenge this confessional constitution; however, the courts have thus far upheld the pastor's right to hold in confidence those things that are shared in a confessional-type manner. The subject naturally leads to the issue of testifying.

Testifying in Court

It is hoped that you will never have to testify in any case in court, but you may. There are a couple of things that may help you if this happens to fall in your lap. You can testify only about what you know firsthand. In our ministry we accept a lot of things, including our own discernment about people, and make decisions based on that information. We make public statements about people's character and commitment to Christian ethics. However, we must avoid being influenced by family members or suspects to say anything that we do not absolutely know to be true.

When I was a chaplain at the jail, it was amazing to me the number of people who came to me to try to convince me how good they were. As it was, jail chaplains were not allowed to testify on behalf of inmates, so there was nothing I could do whether I believed them or not. Since they did not know that, they came to me with all kinds of stories and attempted to convince me that they were of preferable character so that I could report it in court. A pastor's testimony can be very influential, so inmates wanted to use me to their advantage. After I listened to their stories and saw where they were coming from, I would say to them that jail chaplains were not allowed to testify. Sometimes their reaction to my saying this made me very happy that I could not testify in their behalf.

The other thing to remember is that your testimony is merely one thread in a larger fabric. Do not take responsibility for the entire process. As you want the court to be open to hearing your version of the truth, stay open to hearing and learning things you may not know about the person in other aspects of his or her life. It is very true that some people are capable of fooling everybody, and there are times that we may never know the truth. Fortunately, the pastor is not the judge whose job it is to determine guilt or innocence and ultimately to deliver the sentence. The pastor's responsibility is to show mercy, love, and hope to all persons involved.

RESOURCES

Sometimes after we do all that we can do, the persons we love and care for the most wind up in prison. All of the resources we bring to bear on the situation are not sufficient to stop this process from ending in the way it does. I speak now not only from theory, but from personal experience. My one and only son was jailed, released on bond, and rejailed. He went through the trial, was sentenced, and spent time in prison. I can't say what other parents go through when their loved ones are incarcerated, but I know it was very, very painful for me. It was embarrassing. I was angry, I was hurt, and most of all I was powerless. I flirted with a little guilt from time to time, but eventually I was able to throw it off.

First of all, I used all of my relational skills to get him out of jail, but he violated his bond and had to go back. His lawyer said there was no way he could avoid going to prison, but again I used my relational skills and my ministerial influence, and I was able to get him probation. Unfortunately, he violated his probation and still had to go to prison. I share this only for one purpose: as horrid as prison is, there is grace even in prison. I had done all I could to help my son and keep him from going to prison; others as well had talked to him and done all they could to keep him from going. But, like the prodigal son, some people have to learn on their own, and nothing but their own experience will teach them what they need to know.

I learned later that prison was where my son needed to be, because even in prison he misbehaved. He disobeyed the rules; he got into fights; he smarted off to the officers; and he generally took out his anger on the world. It was not the letters that I wrote to him that turned him around; it was not the times I went to visit him that made the difference; it was not the Bible I sent him that he said he read every day; it was not the love of the other family members that turned him around. In his own words, the one who really was responsible for changing his whole attitude about life was an older inmate, a man about forty years old.

As a veteran inmate, this older man knew better than to interfere in anybody else's life or behavior. But for some reason he took it upon himself to speak directly to my son. He was old enough to call my son "boy" and get away with it. And this is what my son reported him saying: "Boy, what are you doing in here? You got no business in here. You're not even like these other guys. The stuff they laugh about, you don't laugh about. The things they think about, you don't even think about. They are never going to do anything with their lives, but you are going to do something with your life. You didn't come from where they came from. And I don't know what you're trying to prove, and who you are trying to prove it to. You're trying to prove something to a bunch of inmates! You better get your act together and get yourself out of here!"

My son listened to what the man had to say and took it in. He said that when he prayed that night there was sincerity in his prayer. He asked the Lord to turn him around. It was at that point that he began to go to school in prison and to try to make the most of his time he had to put in. I had been encouraging him to do this through my letters for sometime, but it had obviously fallen on deaf ears. When my son was released, he was a different person. He is now married, has a beautiful home and three children, and works every day. We now live in two different states. And we have the utmost respect and love for each other.

I say this to those of you who do prison ministry and those who pastor those who may be headed that way. Sometimes the resources that we need to help turn people around are where we least expect to find them. It is not that our voice carries so much weight, or that our title opens doors for us, or that our role is so significant in a particular process, or even that we develop the best relating skills. Sometimes the only thing that does any good is being faithful to our calling, prayerful in our approach, and hopeful of God's mercy and grace in whatever place and through whomever God chooses to manifest God's presence.

I didn't want my son to go to prison any more than I would want him to have open-heart surgery or a leg amputation. But I knew what I had instilled in him as he was growing up; and between that and the prayers of all of those who loved him, the process worked. There may be someone in your church, your family, or your community who you invest yourself in with all your heart, only to be disappointed and frustrated that the end result is not what you had hoped it would be. Don't be so quick to think that your ministry has failed or that God has abandoned you in your prayers. My son later told me that it was a good thing that he went to prison. He said that if he had remained on the street with the anger that he felt, he was sure that he would have killed somebody or somebody would have killed him.

I spent a couple of days with my son's youngest daughter not long ago. She is only five years old, but she walked three miles with me to a restaurant. We have not been able to spend a lot of time together during her life, but she knows me and loves me very much. She trusted me for the whole three-mile walk. These feelings and attitudes she has toward me she learned from her father. She was so proud to be with the man that her father looks up to. Jails and prisons are another world for pastors, but God lives there, too.